F*ck Anxiety

F**ck Anxiety

101 hands-on ways
to soothe anxiety, stop the panic
+ get back to your badass self

Lauren Douglas

Andrews McMeel
PUBLISHING®

The health advice presented in this book is intended only as an informative resource guide to help you make informed decisions; it is not meant to replace the advice of a professional or to serve as a guide to self-treatment. Always seek competent medical help for any health condition or if there is any question about the appropriateness of a procedure or health recommendation.

23 24 25 26 27 RLP 10 9 8 7 6 5 4 3 2

ISBN: 978-1-5248-7058-4
Library of Congress Control Number: 2021947202
www.andrewsmcmeel.com

ATTENTION: SCHOOLS AND BUSINESSES
Andrews McMeel books are available at quantity discounts with bulk purchase for educational, business, or sales promotional use. For information, please write to: Special Sales Department, Andrews McMeel Publishing, LLC, 1130 Walnut Street, Kansas City, Missouri, 64106, or e-mail sales@amuniversal.com.

FOR CAROLINA, SISTER IN ALL THINGS,
EVEN THE SCARIES.
AND FOR CLAIRE, THE DAZZLING
THERAPIST EVERY WOMAN DESERVES.

CONT

ENTS

PART TWO
build + flex your anti-anxiety powers on the daily

Welcome!
You're Safe Here.

First things first: you're a fucking lovely human being. Secondly, you're super safe here. And you're going to survive this, whatever it is. Not because we just wish it to be true, but because that beautiful body of yours can heal from anything. That's science. And you don't fuck with science. Plus, in your hands right now you have 101 research-backed ways to start soothing all your hurting spots.

Try to reach for these when you feel that first whoosh of anxiety. After all, if you were spurting blood out of your leg, would you try to muscle through one more email? Fuck no. You'd get up, find a first aid kit, and slap on a bandage.

Anxiety is like your whole nervous system bleeding, but we just can't see it. But that doesn't make it any less real than that stabby leg wound. And most of the time, we feel it super intensely. Our stomachs turn and roil. Our breath goes all raggedy. We become a big ol' ball of freak-the-fuck-out, and we have no idea what to do.

So think of this book like the first aid kit you'd run for if you were bleeding. Inside it, there is a whole supply of tools to soothe anxiety and panic. Each one will work for different kinds of anxieties and different days, so choose just one thing that sounds good to you. Which one sounds manageable—sounds like it could help? Do just that one tiny thing. Breathe as much as you can.

And remember that any time you turn to your anxiety, see it, and soothe it, you're teaching yourself to act when you feel afraid. You're teaching yourself that you don't have to give in to your fight/flight/freeze response, and you can, instead, choose to apply a bandage to that wound. Over time, as your body starts to learn that you know how to soothe it, it will start to feel that it is safe.

Of course, the bandages can't stitch up deeper hurts, and you may need additional support like medication or other treatments. For sure, you should turn to page 57 and nail down a dazzling therapist to guide you deeper into those hurting places.

But the reality is: anxiety is a part of life. It's your body's way of saying, "Hey, something isn't right here!" It will always strike when you feel triggered, scared, or out of your comfort zone. And that is super okay. Because hopefully this book will help you see it with clear eyes, so you can thank it for trying to protect you, but also calm it down in a hundred delectable, feel-good ways.

Mmmm. That's that good shit. So are you ready to feel good (or at least a little less bad)?

Part One

kick that anxiety spiral in its scrawny ass

In the middle of an anxiety spiral right this second? We got you! In this section, you'll find plenty of things you can do right now to feel calmer and more grounded, as well as things you can get started on tomorrow for lasting change.

In Chapter One, you'll find a whole first aid kit of clinically proven, shot-in-the-arm ways to soothe your nervous system right away and interrupt unhealthy, very sucky rumination spirals so you can get back into your body in the here and now. (Spoiler alert: you are safe!) Consider this chapter your airplane oxygen mask, and you can bet your ass that you need to put yours on first before even thinking about anyone else.

Having a multi-day meltdown inside your brain? In Chapter Two, we're handing you a mop, and we'll show you some ways to start soaking up and wringing out some of those fears seeping into your life. You'll find exercises and resources you can layer into your everyday life so you can hack away daily at a longer anxiety spiral and build long-term coping skills.

So swaddle yourself up somewhere cozy, sit back, and let us take care of you, one chapter at a time. This is your safe space, and we love that you're here!

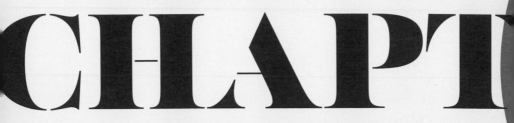

CHAPT

get out of your head

You are here, now!

ER ONE

in ten minutes or less

#1 Notice + Name + Pause

Drop everything you're doing—this is a mandatory vibe check. So, ignore that text. Mute the T.V. Put the snacks down. That shit can wait because you need a minute—this exact minute—to check in with yourself. And that minute starts...right now. Go!

1. **Notice It.** Ask yourself, "How am I feeling right now?" Frustrated? That's alright. Sad? Okay. On the verge of punching a few dumb people in their dumb faces? Fantastic. Embrace those feelings like the validation queen you are.

2. **Name It.** Speak your truth. Point out exactly what's irking you (an emotion, a thought, a person) and say it. Like, out loud. Even if it feels completely weird. Even if you have to mumble it under your breath because the cause of your Big, Bad Feelings is standing, oh, two feet away. This is your moment to call out the bullshit. Call it, girl, call it.

3. **Pause.** Breathe in. Count to ten. Breathe out. Repeat until the screaming in your head goes from an 11 to a manageable 6 or 7. Now that you're somewhat re-centered and can actually think in complete sentences again, check back in with the feels. Still stressed out the wazoo? Skip this rest of this section and hightail it to page 20, where we'll get you back in your body and right mind, STAT.

Feeling calm enough to think actual thoughts? Then read the fancy box below, where we get science-y, because everyone knows that science is the best way to punch your problems in the face.

Science for the Post-Spiral Mind

"Anxiety spiral." "Catastrophic thinking." "Magnifying." Whatever the hell you want to call it, this anxiety gremlin is that one jerk on the mountain that kicks the wrong spot and triggers an avalanche of crappy thoughts. It will convince you that one missed deadline will derail your future or that a poor choice of emoji will end a relationship (hug emoji for you, right here, right now, for that). The spiral is a valid mood, but that doesn't mean you have to let it run the show.

If your body was a car, anxiety might be along for the ride, but it shouldn't get to drive. In fact, it doesn't even have a license, and for all we know, it could be piss-drunk, it's behaving so irrationally! We just cannot trust that guy. Instead, you have the right and the power to take back the wheel, and these are some helpful facts and tips to keep your beautiful booty in that driver's seat.

First, we must know the enemy to defeat the enemy. (Now is an appropriate time to mentally put on your Wonder Woman suit and get real determined.) Anxiety spirals happen when the mind fixates on a set of thoughts so intensely that they trigger a physical response. In other words, your brain psychs itself out so badly that your body goes nuclear and jumps into fight-or-flight-or-freeze mode. Physiologists categorize this response as "hyperarousal," but there's nothing sexy about sweaty palms and overwhelming dread.

So, what's the first line of defense against a literal, living nightmare? Ironically, the source of all your problems: your brain. The brain is like a muscle, and mindfulness is strength training for that muscle (in fact, brain scans suggest that mindfulness can physically change the brain's shape). Practicing mindfulness techniques, like the Notice + Name + Pause practice you just did, helps you monitor your mental state and develop your mental control. These exercises heighten your ability to identify thought patterns or emotional triggers that influence nearly everything about the way you think, speak, and behave.

And, if you notice with your newfound mindfulness powers that you are totally freaking out, that's your cue to use a grounding exercise. You know those cheesy soap operas where someone slaps the hysterical, jabbering character who's having a meltdown, and then suddenly that character is totally themselves again? That's basically what grounding techniques are but less violent and dramatic (unless you're into that?). Grounding is the bitch-slap back to physical reality you need to nip an anxiety spiral in the bud. Together, noticing the start of a spiral + grounding are a powerful wakeup call to pay attention, grab the wheel away from your drunk frenemy, anxiety, and decide for your own damn self just where you'll be heading off to today.

17

#2 Triggered and Frozen? Try This

Can't even right now? That's okay. Sometimes we're so paralyzed by anxiety that the thought of moving even an inch feels like too much. But here's a story: that is normal. That is your body doing what it's supposed to do: protect you. Because it really likes you. It's like the kindly crossing guard of your life, and will it let you get steamrolled by a blazing-by threat? Hell no.

But sometimes our body perceives things that aren't threats—like a cute kitten crossing the road—as big, blaring-red, stoplight threats. That just means you've made an association between that thing or situation and a negative experience. This is a conditioned fear response, aka a trigger. Also, totally normal.

You might have an overactive fear response if you've experienced any kind of trauma (which can be treated and healed—talk to your therapist about all the different trauma modalities!) or if you have anxiety. But we don't need to mentally berate ourselves for freaking the fuck out—yelling at someone who is freaking out works zero percent of the time, right?

Instead, we can help our body work through that fear response by not staying stuck in freeze mode and instead "surviving" that "threat" (the kitten we're perceiving as a slobbery, hungry lion). Yes, you could also fight as a survival tactic, but the drawbacks are that punching kittens is mean, and you might make the real-life situation worse.

So that's what we're going to learn to do here. Next time your brain and body get hijacked by the flight-fight-freeze response, we're going to show them that they can keep themselves safe and get the fuck outta Dodge when they need to.

DO THIS WHEN YOU GOTTA DIP

1. Take a deep breath.
2. And another.
3. One more.
4. Place your feet flat on the floor.
5. Take another deep breath.
6. Stand up.
7. Move your feet until you're walking.
8. Focus on a point across the room, and focus on each step you take to get there.
9. You made it!
10. Keep walking around, focusing on taking a deep breath with each step.
11. Keep going until you feel a little calmer, no matter how long it takes. Everything else can wait—feeling safe is always the first priority.

19

#3 The 54321 Technique

When anxiety comes bull-rushing at you, it can snap you out of your life and into the whirlwind of your mind. Suddenly, your eyes glaze over, your breath catches, your body freezes, and you exist entirely in the hairy and horrifying world of your anxious thoughts. This actually happens on a biological level, says science. A 2017 study found that emotion has a significant impact on our perception, attention, learning, memory, reasoning, and problem solving. So, basically everything that separates us from the toadstools gets kicked offline when anxiety rings the alarm.

Yes, emotions like fear and worry are so powerful that they can turn us into metaphorical bumps on a log. But oddly enough, the fix for this kind of freak-out isn't to address and solve each of those fears. It's to remember that they're fake! Fake like Barbie's pointy, plastic feet. Fake like the Easter Bunny (RIP, old friend). Those fears are nothing but electrical pulses in your brain, triggered by the past or the future, but they are not your reality in this moment.

So anytime you feel yourself disassociated from the present like this, try the 54321 Technique to lurch yourself back to Here and Now. This technique is a tried-and-true favorite of therapists since it can help snap you back to reality (where you are actually safe and still breathing!) in just five quick minutes, no matter where you are.

NINE STEPS TO SNAP BACK TO REALITY

1. Close your eyes.
2. Take two deep, slow breaths.
3. Open your eyes and look around. Out loud or in your head, do the following:
4. Name five things you can see.
5. Name four things you can feel with your body.
6. Name three things you can hear.
7. Name two things you can smell.
8. Name one thing you can taste (take a bite of something, if possible).
9. Take a deep, slow breath to end.

You Are So Here, So Now

Hey! You're here. It's now. Welcome! Yep, this is you, looking at this book and reading this exact sentence. Meta, isn't it? You're probably wondering how you got here, and the answer is simple: you're here! And it's right now. Don't ask questions of the time-warp universe we live in.

When we're fighting off anxiety, it's easy to forget that you are the narrator and the star of this sitcom blockbuster called Your Life. It's all happening right now. The only moment you have is this exact moment. Everything else exists in your head. Trippy shit, right? So this journal space is dedicated to capturing you in this iconic freeze-frame moment.

Let's start by listing the facts, like your name and location. Then explain what you're doing (chilling on the couch, drinking your fourth cold brew, picking up a nearby pen with your foot, etc.). If you're into it, keep going! Give Michelle Obama a run for her money and write your first memoir if that's the mood. We provided the first line with a few blanks to get you started, but no need to mention us in the acknowledgments.

My name is _____, and I live in _____.
The time is _____, and I am currently doing _____.

_____

_____

You are
here,
now,
in your
beautiful
body.

#5 An I-Spy Game for Anytime, Anywhere

Anxiety hits us like the angsty climax from a teen movie: the crap hits the fan, the storm clouds rumble in, and the background details are sacrificed to get an up-close shot of the movie's leading character, Shitty Emotions. The drama sweeps you up in the moment so fully that you forget that you are the director of this whole shit-show, and it's your motherfuckin' story.

But you can reframe the scene just by naming the details of the world around you. It's like playing I Spy, the classic '90s spot-the-thing game, but in real life. This grounding technique works like many others in that it helps you snap back to the Right Here, Right Now, so you can see that you are safe in this moment, even if your mind is trying to convince you it's not. It may feel silly to describe a space out loud, but do you think a directorial genius like Sofia Coppola gave a damn when detailing her vision? Hell no!

So let's pretend we're surveying the scene of the movie of our life and seeing what's here. Start by naming things of the same color. If you don't feel like looking for colors, then try the same exercise with a different category. You're in the director's chair and you know what details will work best to pop your reality back into focus.

I SPY EVERYTHING GREEN

1. Scan the room for one green object.

2. Say what the object is out loud. Don't know what the object is called? Give it a name! In this exercise, every green watchamadoodle gets labeled once and for all.

3. Look for the next green item and name it. Before moving on, compare it to the last object. Is this one darker than the other? How are the surfaces different?

4. If you run out of green, go outside and soak in the view. Try to be as specific as possible. See a tree? Great! What part of the tree is green? A leaf. What kind of green leaf is it? A green oak leaf. Let this exercise be a game where you figure out the most specific name possible for an object. Dig deep in your mental palette to identify the shades of chartreuse, seafoam, emerald, mint, and every other green-ish word you can think of.

5. Keep naming things until you feel reconnected to the environment and greener than kale, avocados, and a green smoothie. With a metal straw, of course.

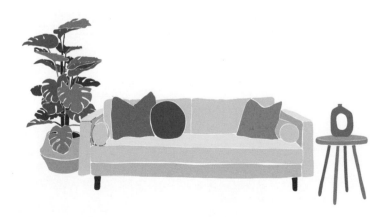

#6 How to Tell Stress to Go Fuck Itself

Fact One: You're here because you're trying to tell your stress to go fuck itself. Fact Two: You want to skip the small talk and fast-track right to the "FUCK YOU, YOU FUCKING FUCKER" part. Fact Three: You flipped to the right section—let's go!

WASH IT DOWN THE DRAIN

1. Turn on a faucet and stick your hands under warm water.
2. Focus on the temperature. Think about the sensation of the water running over your palms and fingers. Go with the flow and imagine rinsing all those angry/sad/scared thoughts down the drain.
3. Switch to cold water. Pay attention to the changes in sensation. How does it feel?
4. Go back to warm. Savor that cozy feeling of warming up.
5. Alternate between warm and cold water until you feel like you're completely focused on the water and present in the moment.

MELT IT AWAY

1. Hold a piece of ice in your hand. Try to take in every detail. Look at its clarity or opaqueness. What is it shaped like? Maybe it's curved with a smooth side or chipped and jagged. Is it refreshingly chilly or something else?

2. Notice how the ice changes as it melts. How is its shape conforming to your hand? Feel the water coat your palm and warm up to the temperature of your hand. Listen to the water droplets fall from your fingers.

3. Watch the ice cube until it's completely gone. If it feels like walking to Mars and back would take less time than waiting for this damn ice to melt, then you're doing it right. You're noticing every single moment and hitting "block" on any other thoughts.

WALK IT OUT

1. Stand up. Notice the pressure on the soles of your feet. If they're feeling a little sore, feel free to skip the walk and try out a foot massage from page 31. This is *your* time, child, and you deserve to do whatever will make you happiest.

2. Take a second to stretch. Enjoy the slight tingle in your joints and muscles.

3. As you start walking, feel your weight shifting from side to side and from heel to toe.

4. Try kicking off your shoes and slowing your pace. Use this moment to really experience the texture of the floor.

5. Feeling stuck? Take it outside! If you can, go barefoot and enjoy the sponginess of the earth or the graininess of the concrete. Bored of focusing on your feet? Give the air a sniff and work in a breathing exercise. Look around you and pick out three small but delightful details. Use your senses to connect to this fresh environment and live in this pocket of peace that you made all by yourself.

How to Hide from the Bullshit

Do you ever get so damn frustrated that you have to bust out a facepalm to shield yourself from the idiots around you? Fantastic! You've almost mastered the relaxation technique of eye-palming already. You are so close to escaping to a better, inner world for a few minutes.

For your brain, covering your eyes is like closing the blinds in your windows. It blocks out the activity outside and further separates your inner space from the outer bullshit. On a biological level, palming the eyes reduces stimuli that activate the sympathetic nervous system (aka the paranoid jerk in your brain that's in charge of the body's panic button). Palming also doubles as a grounding exercise that re-centers your focus back to your body. So try this even if the turmoil is inner, not outer, as even just a quickie break from stimuli can help you feel less overwhelmed.

A QUICKIE BREAK FROM SHITTY SHIT

1. Sit with a straight back and neck. Straight alignment lets blood flow easily.
2. Place your elbows on a flat surface and get comfortable.
3. Rub your hands together or run them under warm water.
4. Line up the bases of the left and right pinky fingers. Then separate your palms to form an inverted "V" under your pinky fingers.

5. Cover your eyes with the V framing the bridge of your nose.

6. Check your form. Your hands should block out any light and rest gently on your face. Reposition your hands if light pokes through or if you feel yourself pushing against your eyes and it feels like too much.

7. Shut your eyes and breathe evenly. Try using a breathing exercise from page 48 to deepen your breath.

8. Let your mind go silent. Visualize a blank surface to help you focus.

9. Hold for as long as you need.

10. With your eyes still closed, remove one finger at a time to slowly reintroduce the light. Open your eyes.

#8 A Fun Game for Un-Fun Times

Here's a blast from the past: Who remembers that hand-clapping game called Concentration? You'd start the game by singing "Concentration, sixty-four, no repeats, or hesitations . . . " and then you'd list all the shit you could think of in a category while keeping a rhythm.

Concentration is basically the perfect grounding exercise because it channels our mental energy into completing a specific task that engages our creativity, vocabulary, memory, and recall speed. And when our brain is juggling all of these functions, it gets stupidly difficult to spare any fucks for anxious thinking. So, pick three categories below and get listing! Try upping the challenge and set a time limit, or list things backward alphabetically. And if you're feeling social, invite a friend—whoever hesitates first has to ~~take a shot~~ engage in a healthy, responsible behavior!

Marine Life	Plants	Pizza Toppings
Movies	Fruits	Things That Are Blue
———————	———————	———————
———————	———————	———————
———————	———————	———————
———————	———————	———————
———————	———————	———————

The Best Masseuse on the Planet is You

Raise your hand if you remember how annoying it was to listen to a scratched CD. (Yes! Retro sisters unite!). And do you remember rubbing the disc on your shirt, popping it back in, and—boom—rocking out again like nothing ever happened?

Well, anxiety is a lot like that scratch. It messes with your jam, but you can rub out that scrape that's screwing with your bop. (Yes, we said "bop." You were warned this would get retro.) Since anxiety comes from the mind, shifting your focus to a physical sensation is just like interrupting the jacked-up music, restarting the disc, and getting back your rhythm.

Too stressed to even know where to start? Try sending some love and attention to those sweet feet. After all, they're always there, you walk on them all day, and they could use a little love, don't you think?

Wiggle your toes. Even if they're in shoes and you're sitting at a desk, you can still focus your attention on how each toe feels wiggling around in your shoe.

If you're wearing shoes, pay attention to the way that particular pair of shoes hugs your feet or maybe pinches your second toe.

If you can, take those shoes right off. Enjoy. That. Freedom. Heaven is a barefoot, bullshit-less day.

Notice what you're standing on. Feel the coolness of the floor or the softness of the rug. Walk around, if you can, and see how your feet feel on different surfaces.

Another reason why your feet deserve appreciation? They're packed with pressure points that affect other parts of the body. Reflexologists see a good ol' foot massage as the cure-all to everything from arthritis, sinus issues, and—you guessed it—stress and anxiety. Basically, your foot's happiness is your happiness.

So, show them some much-deserved TLC and give them a squeeze. And yes, totally, you can do all these same things with your hands instead, if you're just not feeling the feet thing or you're in a setting where rubbing your feet might lead you to freak out about whether people will think you're a freak. Not what we're going for here, so listen to yourself about what feels good.

THREE MINI MASSAGES TO BE YOUR OWN SEXY SWEDISH MASSEUSE

Press Against the Stress

When you're feeling stressed, you can thank your adrenal gland and all of the damn cortisol it's pumping into your body. Sadly, we don't yet have the tech to rocket the adrenal gland and its twisted idea of fun into outer space. But we can teach it a lesson in another area—the big toe.

1. Find the area below the knuckle of your big toe.

2. Gently press your thumb to this area.

3. As you press and hold, breathe deeply and evenly.

Rub Away the Tension

Breaking news: Anxiety and stress cause muscle tension! We hope you're laughing maniacally while curled up in the fetal position just like us. But in other news, you're over it, and now you're ready to massage away the literal pain in your neck.

1. Beginning at the big toe and moving toward the heel, gently press your thumb into the sole of your foot and make circular motions.

2. At the heel, keep pressing and move up to the inside of the ankle.

3. Keep pressing and use circular motions to work your way back to the big toe, following the side of your foot.

4. Repeat this pattern three times or more.

Squeeze Out the Hand Strain

Typing all day: what does it do? If you answered, "Blow smoke up people's asses for a paycheck," then okay, that's naming a feeling, too! Gold star for being honest about where you are right now. But the other thing typing on a computer or phone all day does is gnarl up your fingers. So let's slowly loosen that death grip on How Fucking Stupid All Humans Are and focus just on the micro-universe of our hands for a few minutes.

1. Stretch the hand and fingers.

2. Rub each finger from base to fingertip. Throw in a very gentle twist or pull if you're feeling spicy.

3. Use your thumb and pointer finger to squeeze the fleshy area above your wrist (the round muscle between the base of your thumb and the beginning of your wrist). Rub up from your wrist to the base of your thumb.

4. Squeeze the web between your thumb and pointer finger several times.

5. Rub your palm with your thumb. Use smooth movements to press back and forth from the wrist to the base of a finger, repeating the movement for each finger.

6. Repeat for the opposite hand.

#10 Sixty Seconds of Good-Ass Breathing

If you search "benefits of meditation" on the internet, you would think that you could cure cancer, gain ten IQ points, and open your third eye just by sitting still for fifteen minutes every day. And maybe you can, but sometimes you just don't have the patience for that shit, right? Being zen is great and all, but you have shit to do, damn it.

When you're short on time but sky-high on stress, try Pranayama breathing, which sounds woo-woo but is actually super simple. Pranayama is a breathing technique that can be used as a short meditation break. Best part: "prana" means "life force" and "ayama" means "extend," so this exercise will literally give you life.* The goal is simple: reduce the number of breaths taken in a minute. The average person takes fifteen to twenty every sixty seconds, but we're going to bring that number down to six.

HOW TO BREATHE YOUR WAY TO YOUR 120TH BIRTHDAY (OR JUST REDUCE ANXIETY)

1. Sit with your spine straight. You can also do this lying down, if that helps you focus.
2. Before starting the exercise, breathe in slowly through your nose and out through your mouth. Draw air down into your stomach. You should see your stomach extending with your breath while your shoulders remain still.

3. Pay attention to the different phases of breathing: inhale, retain, exhale, pause. Notice how each one has a varied proportion.

4. With this next practice breath, focus on the exhale. Pranayama is all about sustaining the outgoing air flow.

5. Practice stretching one full breath cycle over ten seconds. Try inhaling for four counts, retaining for two counts, exhaling for six counts, and pausing for two counts.

6. Once you find a pattern that's comfortable for you, listen carefully to the sound of your breathing. You will probably hear a gentle noise, like a "ha," at the end of each breath. Try to finish each cycle as quietly as possible to maximize the peaceful silence between breaths.

7. When you feel like you've got the hang of it, set a timer to sixty seconds and get at it with that serenity thing.

*While technically we cannot prove this, we did our best to believe this fact into existence for you.

35

How to Not Be a Jerk to Yourself

#11

Everyone has a little voice that lives rent-free in their head. Some people think this tiny moocher is a harmless bum, and they are W-R-O-N-G, wrong. People with anxiety (you and me, and probably the whole planet) know that this noisy jerk is actually a highly skilled assassin ready to kill your good vibe with one well-placed toxic thought bomb.

But how the fuck does a literal figment of our imagination have so much influence over our mental health? Psychologists call this internal conversation "self-talk," and before you freak out about having voices in your head, take a breath. Like, a big ol' yoga breath. Because this is totally normal.

Self-talk is so powerful because it's this continuous monologue that tries to make sense of the world around us. So, let's say you're in the bathroom in the morning, looking in the mirror. When your self-talk is mostly positive, you will be more likely to notice your gorgeous flowing hair and feel a little tempted to kiss that goddess in the mirror. But when the mental chatter is leaning negative, your beauty marks may suddenly start looking like blemishes, and that's just not fair to you or Marilyn Monroe.

So, what can you do to redirect your mind back into positive territory? You fight fire with fire! (Yass, burn it DOWN.) And our fire here is going to be some scorching hot affirmations that will be like a flamethrower on all those rude-ass, hater-ade thoughts. Keep these counter-bombs in your back pocket for the next time that really mean voice starts trying to bully you around.

PHRASES TO PUNCH THE HATERS IN YOUR HEAD

- This time is for ME. Anything else can wait for five minutes.
- Things suck right now, but they will get better.
- Everyone struggles with their thoughts and emotions. A lot of people understand what I'm going through.
- Some events are out of my control, and that's just how it is.
- People only remember their own mistakes, not mine. So I can let those memories go.
- Thoughts are not facts. I can change my inner narrative. The only person who can hear the story I'm telling myself is me.
- My support system is always here for me if I want them.

PHRASES TO PEP TALK YOURSELF IN A NON-ANNOYING WAY

- I'm feeling anxious/angry/frustrated/sad right now, and that's okay.
- It's good to take as much time as I need to feel upset. It's part of the healing process.
- It's alright to cry, scream, or punch a pillow sometimes. It helps me get my feelings out of my body.
- I am doing what I can without sacrificing myself, and that is enough.
- I deserve the benefit of the doubt just as much as anyone else does.
- I'm going to cut myself some slack.
- I don't expect other people to be perfect, so I'm not going to expect me to be perfect.

PHRASES FOR BEING
YOUR OWN SOULMATE

- Today, I am choosing to love myself.
- I am proud of myself and my accomplishments.
- I am capable, creative, strong, and an absolute snack.
- My top priority is me.
- I can do this.
- My body is strong and resilient. It deserves some TLC and that extra piece of chocolate.
- I am good, and I am loved.
- I am going to stubbornly, fiercely love myself as a big F-U to the haters.

Should you be WaCkY and say these out loud? You betcha. Your actual, real voice will always be louder than your internal one, so some days you might just have to shout down that mean, sniveling little jerk inside. And yes, talking out loud may feel awkward, but if you lean into the weird and don't take it so seriously, you might even get a laugh or two out of this whole thing. And nothing cuts a jerk down like laughing in his face. Lol, douchebag!

The Easiest Five Minutes of Yoga Ever

#12

If a couch potato and a blanket burrito had a child, it would be me. My cellular composition is 90 percent floofy fabrics and 10 percent whatever else makes humans survive. (Water? Poop? Actual burritos?)

We're all plush comforters at heart . . . HOWEVER, we are also women of science, and our sisters in the science realm are all about the benefits of exercise. (Yes, they are that friend who pushes you to do self-care when you'd rather cry facedown on the couch for three weeks straight.) Research shows that it only takes five minutes of aerobic exercise to reduce anxiety and decrease tension. Active and restorative yoga poses can both check the aerobic box and engage the entire body so that it slowly and surely goes from "!!!!!!!" to "mmm yesss."

If we lost you at "exercise," we respect that dedication to relaxation and raise you a guide to napping on page 162. For everyone else, shimmy into your cutest leggings—we're putting the "athletically-uninclined-but-here-anyway" back into athleisure. Try either this active five-minute or deliciously restorative fifteen-minute yoga sequence to start reaping the benefits without getting all psyched out about the effort.

ACTIVE YOGA

Did you know that some people do yoga instead of drink coffee for their morning boost? (LMAO—we laughed, too.) They recommend this routine for a quick burst of energy, and we recommend bringing a latte for added "support."

Child's Pose

1. Kneel on your mat and sit on your feet with your big toes together.

2. Separate your knees slightly.

3. Place your hands flat on the floor in front of you and begin leaning your torso forward.

4. Slowly walk your hands forward until your arms are stretched out and your forehead touches the floor. You will feel a stretch running from your head to your tailbone.

5. Adjust the pose so that it's comfortable for you. I f you feel tension in your arms or back, don't reach as far foward.

6. Hold for sixty seconds. Use this moment to notice your thoughts and breathe deeply.

Downward-Facing Dog

1. Transition into the next movement by reaching your fully extended arms forward a few more inches and stretch out your fingers.

2. Tuck your toes under and rest on the balls of your feet.

3. Lift your hips up by straightening your legs and flattening your feet to the ground. Your body will look like a mountain with your butt as the mountain's peak.

4. Keep a firm grip on the mat and align your head between your arms. Bend your knees to lessen the burn.

5. Hold for sixty seconds. This stance reinvigorates your muscles and increases blood flow to the brain.

Upward-Facing Dog

1. Next, shift forward into a plank. Your position will look like you just did a push-up.

2. Untuck your toes so the tops of your feet are flat against the mat.

3. Tighten your thigh muscles and glutes.

4. Lower your hips to the ground while trying to keep your thighs off the ground.

5. Curve your chest out and lean your head back.

6. Push your hands down into the mat and gently draw your shoulders down.

7. Keep your core engaged by tightening the muscles in your stomach to lower the back strain.

8. Hold for sixty seconds. Now, you're opening up your chest and increasing activity in the heart and lungs.

Low Lunge

1. Start the low lunge by untucking your toes and moving back into down dog.

2. Swing your right leg forward and plant your right foot in between your hands.

3. Untuck your left foot, place the top of the foot against the mat, and let your left knee slowly come down to the floor.

4. Square off your hips. Bring the left hip forward and draw the right hip back so that there is no twist in your torso.

5. Bend your right knee and lower your hips. The knee will always face forward, like your toes.

6. Breathe deeply and stretch your arms up.

7. Exhale while gently bending your head back, deepening the curve in your back.

8. Hold for thirty seconds. Then place your hands back on either side of your foot.

9. Step your right foot back into downward-facing dog.

10. Repeat for your left leg.

11. Hold for thirty seconds. Low lunges strengthen the hips and increase blood flow to the lower body.

Lotus Pose

1. Sit cross-legged with upright posture.
2. Bring your right foot into the fold of your left knee. Do the same for the opposite leg. If you're not feeling this level of flexibility, keep enjoying that cross-legged position. Do what makes you feel good.
3. Place your hands on your thighs. Face your palms down to ground yourself or turn them up to gain energy.
4. Hold for sixty seconds. This final pose improves posture and is a must for anyone with I-Sit-At-A-Computer-All-Day body aches.
5. Unfold your legs, one foot at a time. If you're enjoying the serenity, take an extra moment to practice some meditation or deep breathing.

RESTORATIVE YOGA

Life should be lived under a blanket, right? Especially if it's an extra-soft blanket. Or a heated blanket. Or a blanket that is also your clothing. Or a blanket that is also your body. (How can we become blankets? Science, answer us!) Luckily, you have one more reason not to emerge from your blanket fort/body, and that is restorative yoga. This very finest and softest kind of yoga gives you a socially acceptable reason to roll around in a warm and fuzzy pile and call it exercise.

Supported Forward Fold

1. Sit with your legs extended in front of you, side by side.
2. Slightly bend your knees up and slide a rolled blanket under them.
3. Take a folded blanket and place it on your legs. The length should run from your stomach to your ankles.

4. Keep your back straight and slowly lean forward onto the blanket. Let your arms rest on either side of your legs.

5. Add more layers to your blanket stack to ease the forward stretch. You should feel elongated and comfortable.

6. Hold this pose and practice deep breathing for five minutes.

Reclining Bound Angel Pose

1. Lie down on your mat and bring your feet together.

2. Bend your knees and draw your heels in close to your bottom.

3. Open your knees to either side and hold the soles of your feet together, like a butterfly stretch.

4. Place pillows or blankets under your knees for support. You should feel a moderate stretch in your inner thighs.

5. Breathe deeply and let your arms rest where they feel comfortable and at ease.

6. Hold for five minutes. Check in with your body and readjust as needed.

Supported Fish Pose

1. Gather long pillows that can stretch from your lower back to the top of your head. You can also use folded blankets.

2. Sit on your mat with legs extended and together.

3. Stack your supports behind you and lean back, keeping your booty and legs flat against the floor.

4. Let your arms rest on either side with your palms facing up.

5. Hold for five minutes and let your mind go quiet.

#13 Straight Spine, Strong Bitch

Here's the thing: I have terrible posture, and I mean TERRIBLE. The Leaning Tower of Pisa is more perpendicular to the earth than I am. And if you work at a computer, or just exist as a human who spends a lot of time on a screen, you're probably a little crooked, too.

While a nice, deep slouch-and-collapse can feel good after a hard day, having poor posture all the time not only screws with your back, but it fucks with your stress hormones. According to Science and Research™, a slouchy posture mimics the defensive stance that is triggered instinctively whenever the body feels threatened. So, you know that moment of fear when your boss randomly ambushes you just to "check in"? Your muscles tense immediately, your shoulders curl in, and your body starts doing its best armadillo impression. To put it scientifically, crooked posture is your body's first response to freaking the fuck out.

How does all this affect anxiety? Basically, poor posture is the green light for all your stress hormones to come running in and set fire to your health and happiness. But good posture? Good posture kicks the stress hormones in the face and says, "NOT ON MY WATCH."

And, because we love a good deal and we love you, we also have happy news: good posture is a two-for-one deal! Good posture reduces stress hormones and it can raise your self-confidence. It keeps the bad out and lets the good in. The secret is power poses or power stances. A power pose is a type of body language that increases confidence and commands attention by intentionally taking up as much space as possible. It's a pose that wordlessly announces, "I'm the baddest bitch around, and I know it." (Middle finger in the air optional.)

In her popular book, *Presence*, social psychologist Amy Cuddy breaks down poses frequently struck by the world's most influential people (we're talking CEOs, presidents, celebrities, and the queen herself, Oprah). She believes that everyone can channel the confidence and authority of the famous and powerful just by imitating their body language. Strike one of these poses and try to remember us when you land that promotion, snag a hottie, and cure cancer next week.

THE SUPERHERO

1. Plant your feet on the ground, hip-width apart.
2. Firmly place your hands on your hips.
3. Take a deep breath in and puff out your chest.
4. Pull your chin up to enhance the stance's power.
5. Hold for two minutes. Manifest the confidence and swag of your favorite spandex-wearing crime-fighter.

THE CORPORATE EXEC

1. Find a seat with a back and sit down.
2. Rest one arm (or both!) along the back of the chair.
3. Embrace the man-spread and space out your knees.
4. Lean back comfortably into the seat.
5. Try putting your hands behind your head or crossing an ankle over your knee for some added spice.
6. Hold two minutes. Get that big exec energy. Elevate your mood. Profit.

THE ROCKSTAR

1. Stand with your feet planted on the ground.

2. Widen your stance past hip-width.

3. Raise your arms above your head and angle them out, so your whole body forms an "X" shape.

4. Keep your posture tall and your chin raised. Remember: you're more than part of this show, you're the motherfuckin' headliner.

5. Hold for two minutes and collect the imaginary bouquets of flowers strewn on your stage.

#12 Four Unsucky Ways to Breathe Deeper

Have you ever been mid-rant, quite possibly giving the best speech in the history of womankind, and the person you're speaking to says, "Hey, calm down and take a deep breath"? First of all, fuck that person. Second of all, that person is completely fucking right. UGH. Annoying, isn't it? But even though taking a breath is probably the last thing on your mind when you're caught in a mental vortex, and being told to take a breath feels like an invitation to go Rage Level 11 on someone, you can always, always give yourself a chance to deflate even when every fiber in your being wants to inflate you up to that next level of fight-or-fight-harder.

We all know that deep breathing can help us feel calmer, but did you know that poor breathing technique can actually add to our physical and emotional destress? Sounds too cruel to be true, yet it is. People start to breathe from their chest when they experience fear or anxiety, taking short and shallow breaths. This type of breathing throws off your oxygen and carbon dioxide levels. Now you're dizzy, tense, and your heart's beating a mile a minute, all of which—guess what—makes you and your body even more stressed!

Sometimes our meat-shells really suck (like, seriously, who's side are you on?!), but remember: you're a badass who's ready to take control and lay down the motherfuckin' law. *Flips down aviator shades and surveys the horizon.* Deep breathing techniques redirect airflow back down into your abdomen and kick-start your parasympathetic system by storing up carbon dioxide. Basically, they're the cheapest chill pills you'll ever find.

BASIC DEEP BREATHING

1. Put your hand on your stomach and breathe deeply through your nose. Your stomach will push your hand out while the rest of your body will stay still.

2. Exhale from your mouth. Relax your jaw and lightly purse your lips. Enjoy the satisfying "whooshing" noise.

3. Repeat for several minutes.

BOX BREATHING

1. Sit upright with your feet planted flat on the ground (imagine a string gently pulling you up from the top of your head). Relax your hands in your lap with your palms facing upward.

2. Slowly exhale all of the oxygen in your lungs. For this step and each going forward, notice how the sensations in your body change along with the airflow.

3. Breathe in through your nose while slowly counting to four in your mind.

4. Hold your breath and slowly count to four again.

5. Exhale over another four counts. Expel all the air from your lungs and stomach.

6. Hold your breath for four counts, then repeat as needed.

50/50 BREATHING

1. Sit comfortably with good posture.
2. Inhale while counting slowly to five.
3. Exhale over the same count to five. The goal is to balance the breath coming in and going out, so you keep track of time however you like. Try silently reciting a list (not a to-do list—don't even think about it!) or bringing in an affirmation.
4. Pause after each inhale and exhale.
5. Repeat for three to five minutes.

BUZZING BEE BREATHING

1. Get into a comfortable sitting position.
2. Let your eyes shut and relax your facial muscles.
3. Find your ears' tragus cartilage (the little triangles that hide your ear canal and hold your earbuds in place).
4. Place your index fingers on the tragus cartilage found on both sides of your head.
5. Breathe in deeply, then press your cartilage gently as you breathe out.
6. As you exhale, close your mouth and hum loudly.
7. Repeat until you feel fully recentered.

The Hype Woman Cometh

Is there one person in your life who thinks you're the hottest shit alive? (If not, let's make space for that person by dumping the actually shitty people—advice on page 68!) Like, if you left them in a room with a stranger, your hype woman would convince this person that you single-handedly discovered the cure for cancer, walked a tightrope over a shark-infested canyon, and dared to wear white pants during your last period. Basically, in their eyes, you are Baddest Bitch incarnate.

We would bet a million dollars that your favorite person believes everything they say about you, AND we would bet another billion dollars that you don't think the same about yourself. But you should, and here's why: your favorite person has 20/20 vision about you, and they see SO much good. So, when loving yourself gets difficult and staying #positive makes you want to puke, let someone else say the nice things for you.

My favorite person would say:

_____

_____

_____

_____

_____

_____

_____

_____

CHAPT

get stubborn against

ER TWO

a longer spiral

#16 Feel Those Feels

Have you ever felt an emotion so intensely that you accidentally activated Hulk-mode and changed into an entirely different person? Last time, I woke up to four empty wine bottles, two ruined friendships, and one smoldering town. For legal reasons, I can't say more.

But have you ever wondered how the hell emotions can make us do stuff we normally would never do, like punch a hole in the wall or text our ex? Scientists who study feels (yes, this is a real field of research) see emotions as an automatic, chemical response to a stimulus. Feelings start happening when the brain notices that chemical reaction and reacts to it. For example, all of the fun stimuli at a New Year's Eve party trigger automatic bursts of dopamine (and the dranks don't slow things down, either). Your brain then translates that dopamine surge into feelings of happiness, elation, and giddiness. So by the time the ball drops, you're so overwhelmed with those warm and fuzzy feels that you make out with the first person you can grab. Yep, you really can blame it on the emotion chemicals pulsing through your veins, not just the juice.

Sure, that's a positive example, but things could have just as easily gone south if the person you grabbed was really regrettable. Then, the feelings of happy that night could have fueled a lot of unhappy the next morning. But here's the tea: emotions aren't "bad" or "good"—they're just chemical-based signals that are doing their thang in your beautiful body. The problem is when those chemicals start running the show and single-handedly motivating actions, because actions have Real-Life Consequences. Uh, does anxiety-fueled destructive behavior ring a bell for anyone?

When it comes to anxiety, it is a must—and we mean A MUST—to remember that the intensity of the feeling does not necessarily reflect reality. And this just in: it's usually not even close! Like, we're talking not even in the same motherfuckin' ballpark. Feelings can be so strong that they hijack your brain and make you lose perspective or do things you don't actually want to do.

But you should be the only one controlling your actions. Not chemicals in your body. So how do you avoid a Big Feels blow-up? You start learning to Name + Notice + Pause. (Go to page 14 for a primer on this!) To slow things down, therapists often teach their clients to name their emotions out loud as a way to reduce the likelihood of a nuclear meltdown at your inner Anxious Energy Plant. Naming emotions helps close the gap between thoughts and feelings, and it reminds us that although, yes, the emotion exists in this moment, it isn't all of reality. Labeling your emotions ultimately helps you see them for what they are—valuable bits of data, but not all of the data—so you can process them alongside everything else you know to be true. To start, it helps to let yourself feel the feeling instead of judging it or numbing it, so you can see it's not quite as terrifying as it seems.

HOW TO FEEL YOUR FEELS

1. Surprising/annoying/scary event happens.

2. You notice that your body is telling you something and say, out loud if possible, "I feel shocked/angry/frightened."

3. Take one deep inhale.

4. Say what your thoughts are. "My thoughts are about how I don't understand this/I'm pissed as hell at that person/I'm scared of what might happen next."

5. Slowly exhale and soften your shoulders or anyplace else where you're tense or clenching. If emotion wells up, let it out. Cry if you need to, punch a pillow if you're angry, or journal if you're reeling and confused. Finding a healthy, nondestructive way to release all that emotional energy is your first priority, so you don't just stuff it down, distract yourself with something else, or unleash it in a way that will make you feel worse later.

6. As you feel all that steam start to peter out, keep slowly inhaling and exhaling, letting your body calm down.

7. Once you feel grounded again, even if it takes hours or a day or two, name how you feel now and remind yourself: I got through that. I can ride the waves of my feels. They are temporary. They don't last forever. And I don't need to make any choices or take any actions when I'm in the midst of a wave—it can all wait.

8. Over time, like a pro surfer, you'll get a little better and kinder with yourself as the waves of Big Feels crash over you, because, hey, you've been here before, and it doesn't last forever. You can survive this.

How to Find a Dazzling Therapist

#17

Anxiety is the Italian sports car of emotions—it takes you from zero to sixty in three seconds and costs a small fortune to maintain. Caring for our mental health demands a fuck-ton of resources but seeing a therapist can be one of your best investment choices. But before you say, "Oh, well my anxiety isn't that bad," think about this: Do you take your car to the mechanic only after a serious accident? No way! You see a pro regularly, because it's their job to Keep. That. Shit. Running.

And just like you wouldn't settle for any schmuck off the street to keep your Lambo running, you shouldn't settle for a therapist that isn't revving your mental fitness engine. But finding your therapist soulmate is an exhausting job, so we've put together a few tips to get you on your way to finding THE ONE.

KNOW YOUR TYPE

Therapists have different specialties, and though there are dozens of modalities, here are two of the most common:

Cognitive-behavioral therapy (CBT): CBT looks for detrimental behaviors and then tries to identify the emotions and beliefs that fuel those habits. The therapist then helps the patient develop healthier thought patterns and regulate emotions so that they can make different choices. The therapist may assign "homework" to help you self-monitor and discover new coping mechanisms.

Psychodynamic therapy (PDT): PDT is the talk-based method that usually comes to mind when we think of stereotypical therapy. You and the therapist will try to better understand your current situation by resolving things in your personal history. This method takes patience, as it is very talk-based.

DATING THE CANDIDATES

Just like with real dating, you won't know if you've found The One until you've met several options. Here are a few strategies for putting yourself out there:

- Start by asking someone you trust for a referral. Ask a close friend or doctor about their experience and recommendations.
- Contact your insurance provider or search online to learn more about specialists in your area. Many websites, like HelpPro, are designed to help you find the right mental health care professional.
- Contact potential therapists. After talking logistics, don't be afraid to ask about their backgrounds (you may feel more comfortable with someone you can identify with, and a good therapist will understand that!).

RED FLAGS

Dealing with anxiety is hard, so your comfort comes first and foremost. Consider these questions when sussing out any weird vibes:

- How do you feel in the space? Does the room seem safe and private? Are there any distractions?
- Do you have the therapist's full attention?
- Do you feel a connection? Your therapist should be someone you trust AND look forward to talking to.

- How do you feel after a session? Do you feel uneasy or confused? Do you feel heard and understood? Remember, you don't have to justify to the reality TV show cameras why you liked or didn't like someone—just go with your gut feeling, even if you can't explain where it came from.

THE FINAL ROSE

You've done the emailing. You've had the first session. You've cut the Not-The-Ones, and now you're ready to make that commitment.

- **Check your insurance.** Contact your provider to go over what is covered and what comes out of pocket. Remember that a good therapist will make you trillions of times happier than a new pair of shoes, so don't shy away from someone you love if you have to pay out of pocket. (Only if you can afford to do that and still eat! Food first, girl.)

- **Discuss your goals.** Once you've landed with someone who gets you, spend a session or two just talking about where you're struggling and where you want to focus your time over the next few months. Remember that these sessions are yours—they're your time to talk about anything you want, so don't feel like you have to go along with a set plan if there's something new and tough you're grappling with that week or month.

- **Commit + stay flexible.** It can be helpful to have weekly sessions the first few months, so you and your therapist can grow a budding new rose of a relationship, but if it needs to be less frequent because of time, money, or just emotionally hitting a wall and needing time to process in between, say so. Just like any time at the gym is better than zero time at the gym, any time in therapy will help you inch closer to where you want to go. But at least therapy lets you sit on a couch, so really—let's be honest—it's better.

BREATHE

Move, #18 Even in a Sloth-y Way

So, here's our take: Scrolling through social media and clicking "Next Episode" burns at least 500 calories per click. There's a lot of nonexistent data to back this up, but since we don't want to bore you with all that science, we'll just get down to it: You should probably get up. And move. At least a little. Like, walking across the room is a good start.

We've already talked about the major benefits of physical activity in Chapter One (TL;DR—exercise bitch-slaps your body out of Freak-Out Mode, and to put it academically, gets us the fuck out of our heads). Movement forces our internal systems to work together and boosts the flow of endorphins, aka the body's in house happiness juice. But stop! Before you buy that trendy, probably overrated, and stupid-expensive workout equipment that will supposedly finally get you to exercise regularly, we need to talk about the difference between fitness and movement.

If you arranged exercise philosophies on a spectrum, fitness and movement practices would fall at opposite ends. Comparing a fitness routine and a movement practice is like comparing your Instagram and your personal journal (one is about you and the other is about the real you). Fitness is all about that A-E-S-T-H-E-T-I-C. She's the woman with a link to a detox tea in her bio and coordinated sports bras and leggings for every day of the week (because duh, she exercises every day, don't you?). She is just as judge-y as she sounds, and we are not here for it.

Movement, on the other hand, is your friend who lives in the real world and says "you do you" so much that it stops being annoying and starts being adorable and validating. A movement practice is rooted in your personal relationship with exercise. (And yes! We do love this journey for you.) While fitness focuses on getting us closer to an ideal number or image, movement uses physical activity to help us reach other goals.

So, one person could do kickboxing to build up their self-defense skills and relieve their pent-up anger so they don't stab every annoying person they work with. Another person might join a dance class to expand their social circle and bring more flow and joy into their lives. Someone else might take up yoga so they can stretch out all that text-neck tension or feel grounded in their bodies after something tough happens.

Whether it's inspired by a Big Scary Thing you're working through or a simple hatred of the Karen from HR, your movement practice should do something for both your body AND your spirit. You might already know what that activity is, and if you do, then get that beautiful booty moving! If you're still searching or just want to try something new, try one of these.

MOVEMENT THAT DOESN'T SUCK

- Does walking around the block bore you to ugly tears? Try walking on a trail in a park (aka "hiking," which sounds so much more exercise-y and rugged than it is) or go "hiking" through the mall. Bonus points if you walk with weights and the weights are shopping bags.
- Plant some tiny tomatoes in a pot, or start a larger plot. Gardening is definitely exercise, plus you get delicious noms out of it.

- Go to the local pool, beach, river, lake, or any other large body of water that you must move in otherwise you'll drown.
- Try racquetball or tennis or kickball or any other game that lets you crush fools while also moving your body.
- Try a few different kinds of yoga, Pilates, barre, or any other studio exercise until you find something you don't shudder at the thought of.
- Give weightlifting at the gym a try, or search online for videos of body weight exercises you can do at home with no equipment and no fucks given about what you look like.
- Clean the house, cook or bake, work on a DIY project, or anything else that involves not sitting but also checks off your productive boxes for that double-wham win.

#19 Boundaries Are the New Black

Hi, and welcome to People Pleasers Anonymous. We like you here. (Do you like us?) Listen, we've all been there. Many of us go through a phase—or lifetime—where we will do anything to make someone happy. Yes, we would spend the weekend helping you move and then drive you across the country. And sure, we would take on that extra part of the project because who really needs seven hours of sleep every day? "Not us!" we said while melting into a puddle of drool deep inside.

At the peak of any Yes-To-Anything crisis, your popularity will be at an all-time high, just like your anxiety levels! But it's worth it to see everyone so happy . . . is the bullshit we all tell ourselves before we finally discover this revolutionary concept called "setting boundaries." Boundaries are about separation and division, and that's why they're so fucking amazeballs. If you were a snack (and we know you are *wink wink*), a boundary is the reusable baggie that keeps you in snackable condition and protects you from All-That-Other-Shit. Besides sealing in your freshness, boundaries preserve your time and your freedom from all the little moochers that are vying to get a piece of you. Essentially, drawing these lines defines where the world's demands end and your needs begin.

Establishing healthy boundaries can be A Big Scary Thing, especially when "assertive" is not your middle name; however, they are essential for traversing the anxiety landmine known as Life. It will take a lot of self-awareness to learn what yours are, and it'll take a butt-load of resolve if you want to protect those new boundaries. But we're not here to build the fucking Great Wall of China in one day. Right now, our goal is to help you put your sexy snack self back in that baggie and make that wrapping impermeable again.

BOUNDARY-SETTING 101

Prioritize yourself.

Before you even think about starting this process, you have to give yourself permission to say, "This is for me." Acknowledging that your feelings and needs deserve their own space will motivate you to stick by your guns when it's tempting to just say "yes."

Define your limits.

Effective boundaries separate the "yeah, I can handle this right now" from the "aww, fuuccckkkk, please save me." When finding yours, you'll identify what is tolerable and what stresses you the fuck out. The best way to do this is to reflect on your past and think about what changes you want to see in the future. These limits may look like:

- I will stop bringing work home, because I want to enjoy my personal life and keep it separate from my job.
- My social media accounts are set on "private" because I want to connect with my friends and loved ones, not my ex from five years ago or my lab partner from high school.
- I will be accountable for my own mistakes, but not ANY mistake. I will not be responsible for or apologize for other people's actions.
- Saturday mornings are for me and only me. Anything that wants my attention can wait until my facemask and my weekend cartoons are done.

Keep it short and sweet ... or just say "Fuck no!"

Let's get one thing straight: Saying "no" isn't selfish. It is a form of self-respect and self-care. "No" defines and reinforces the limits you establish. People who understand and respect your choices won't expect you to explain yourself, make apologies, or find excuses. It's the people who benefited from you having no boundaries—who liked that you used to do whatever they wanted—who are the ones most likely to get pissy once you start setting them.

If you feel like you are having to over-explain your boundary, you may want to reconsider your relationship with that person and ask, "Is this relationship healthy and reciprocal?" Remember that the most important relationship in your life is with you, so sometimes you have to Tiger-Mom-fierce-protect your own damn self.

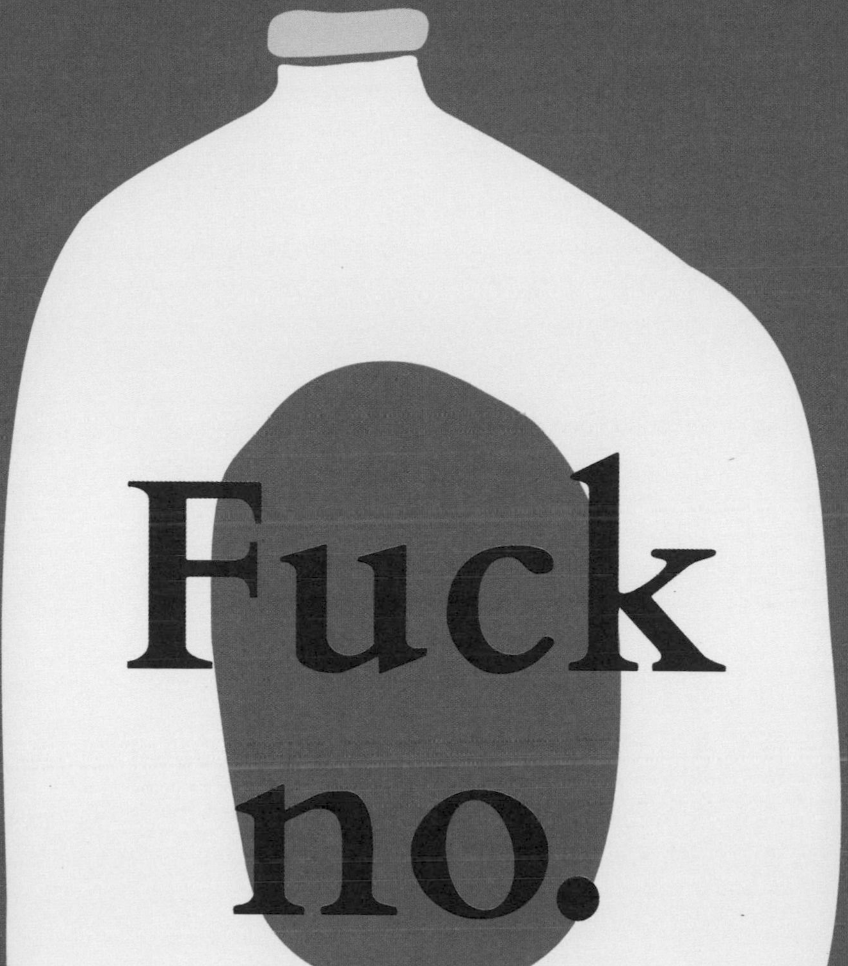
Fuck
no.

#20 Dump Toxic-Ass People

Let's not fuck around: Toxic People are the bedbugs of your life, and they must be eradicated. These are the creepy-crawly coworkers, in-laws, and longtime "friends" who you absolutely dread running into because they make you queasy or uneasy. And just like actual pests, they mooch off you whenever possible and scuttle away whenever you try to shine light on the situation.

This invasive species wheedles into our physical and emotional space to fulfill their needs because toxicity is all about taking. Toxic relationships can manifest through constant nagging, drama, judgment, lying, or any other behavior that radiates high school mean-girls vibes. Basically, toxic people are the kryptonite to your superhuman strength, and that shit needs to be hermetically sealed and launched into outer space, and fast.

Well, today we're putting on our hazmat suits and dragging out the toxic waste bins because we're sorting through this human rubbish pile and taking out the fucking trash.

TIME TO TAKE OUT THE FUCKING TRASH

1. Start by writing down all the draining people in your life. Who, when you remember their name, makes you cringe a little, or gives you a twinge of a negative feeling? Once you've taken stock of the garbage around you, divide it into a "cut-all-ties" pile, a "limit-exposure-whenever-possible," and a "test for toxicity" pile.

2. For the "cut-all-ties" pile, DO IT. Unfollow, block, delete their number, take them off your Christmas card mailing list, and say it with me now: they don't deserve your attention (*finger-snap*).

3. The "limit-exposure-whenever-possible" pile includes people like your desk neighbor or mother-in-law—you could avoid them but getting a new job/husband/life in Mexico seems like a lot of work. So instead, write down exactly when and why you have to interact with them and limit all interactions to that bubble. What circles of trust will you let them into: finances, relationships, work, etc? What will you talk to them about, and what things are totally off the table? Getting clear on what parts of your life they're allowed into will help you keep them at a safe, sanity-saving distance.

4. The people in the "test for toxicity" pile are trickier—they have some redeeming qualities but can get soul-sucking in a snap. (But hey, every human has a dash of toxic in them.) So you're going to start collecting data on where these people are forces for good and where they're forces for freak-out in your life. Jot this down in your phone when you're with them or right after a hang. Things like, "Had so much fun, but not cool when she made comments about my body." Then, next time this fixer-upper of a friend does The Rude Thing, gently and kindly tell them how it makes you feel. (See page 64 for help with boundaries!) If they get it and make an effort to stop, hooray! If not, back into pile #1 or #2 for them.

#21 Beep, Beep, You Are Not a Robot

If you're anything like us, then you're fueled by three things: coffee, pizza, and the burning desire to do everything flawlessly on the first try. Not only do we anxious people come from the same robot factory, but we share the same, singular directive: ACHIEVE PERFECTION (SFX sparkles). And anything that falls short of this goal spits out error code 102: DOES NOT COMPUTE. Or, as the humans would say, "That makes no fucking sense."

Besides the suffocating pressure to succeed, life as a humanoid perfection-bot is simple . . . at least until you run the Human_Emotions_and_Imperfecti0ns.zip file for the first time. Suddenly you see this glitch called mistakes, and you're caught in a whirlwind of self-criticism, guilt, and disappointment. Even worse, you're finally slapped in the face with a truth colder than your metallic heart: You're actually a giant network of complex thoughts and feelings. You are a HUMAN, not a robot (cue cascade of error dialogue boxes and angry beeping).

Grappling with anxiety and perfectionism is more than a struggle—it's the textbook example of a giant-ass toxic relationship. Therapists say that anxious people sometimes chase after perfection as a way to cope with their anxiety (if you're perfect, you can't fail and everyone will love you forever and ever, right?). But the pressure to perform only leads to more procrastination, exhaustion, risk-aversion, and self-judgment, aka the Four Horseman of the Stress Apocalypse. In other words, your Stress Beast is a very hungry hippo, and you are the motherfucking all-you-can-eat buffet.

So, where do you even start the perfectionism deprogramming process? Well, start by pouring yourself some wine or kombucha, because we're about to get cheesy as hell: step one is acknowledging that you have a problem. Welcome to our support group—it's just as sitcom-y dopey yet life-changing as you'd expect. And wait! We know it's incomprehensible, so *deep breath in* say it with us: "Admitting that I have a problem is a sign of strength and self-love." Opening yourself up to this vulnerable space can be the hardest part for us weathered perfectionism robots. It's realizing that what we thought was our cool metal robot armor is actually just a cardboard box we spray-painted silver and glued some buttons on. But accepting your humanness starts here and continues with these practices below.

HOW TO EMBRACE
YOUR HUMANNESS

Name Your Intention.

Before you can set out on your #journey, you have to know what your end goal is. Learning to accept yourself and your humanness is the same. Setting your intention can be as broad as staying open to more tolerance and trust, or it can be as specific as saying, "I will cultivate self-acceptance instead of self-hatred."

Whichever path you take, write the one or two key words you're working toward in a spot that you'll see often, since it's easy to switch on auto-pilot and run our outdated old software when stress gets too high.

Resist Your Inner Critic.

We've talked about the voices in our head (reminder: it's totally normal!), but your Inner Critic takes the crown for Most Obnoxious Piece of Shit. This loudmouth poses as your voice of reason, but its "truth" is nothing but harsh and untrue judgment. We talk about blocking out the haters Out There, but we overlook this jerk In Here constantly.

That's why it's important to start calling out and turning down the volume on your inner critic, because its only purpose is to drag you down. It does not have the final say on what is reality, no matter how much it thinks it does. When you feel it clawing its way to the front, kindly remind yourself that you are only human and all you can do is try to keep learning, damn it.

Practice Self-Forgiveness.

Even if you're not a perfectionist, most of us hang on to our past guilt and regrets like the leg warmers that we swear will come back into fashion (I'm sorry, but they won't, let it go). But letting go makes more room in our literal and metaphorical closets for better investments, like self-acceptance and growing from our mistakes. As much as we think that berating ourselves for our failings is the best way to grow, the true, starry-sky, big universe reality is that forgiving ourselves is how we actually change and grow.

So go ahead. Pick up that package of forgiveness that's sitting right in front of you. It's a free gift, and it's yours, if you'll just tear off the wrapping and bask in its goodness. (And it never goes out of style! And it looks so good on you, girl.)

Say No to Murder; Say Yes to Being Blessed

#22

All of us have heard that showing gratitude absolutely slaps, but did you know that it literally changes the shape of your brain, makes you happier, and makes you less likely to murder people who annoy you? It's Homicide Prevention 101!

One study with over 300 participants showed that people who were told to keep a regular gratitude journal reported higher levels of optimism and happiness by the end of the ten-week period. Practicing gratitude is so crazy-effective because it forces us to see that there's Good Stuff right alongside the Tough Stuff. Like, how can you fixate on your one flub from middle school (which PSA, literally no one remembers) when you're remembering how your friend gifted you part of their mind-blowingly delicious strawberry and unicorn-sprinkle donut? Even in the darkest moments, there's still a unicorn-sprinkle donut out there for you.

So no matter how mucky or barf-inducing your day has been, taking two minutes to remember what was good is the reminder you need that, hey, not every last thing sucks. If you're ready to look at the bright side of life, put on your darkest shades and prepare to stare into the fucking Gratitude Sun with these five thankfulness practices.

FIVE QUICK WAYS TO SPRINKLE SOME GRATITUDE SPARKLES ON YOUR DAY

1. **Remember your blessings.** Yes, you are blessed, you cheesy little cheese puff, you. Take two minutes, anytime during the day, to jot down three things you're grateful for. Or, set aside time on Sunday to look back on bigger things over the past week that were bright and sparkly. You can even tap this list out on your phone the next time you're stuck in line or in a slump or spiral. Anything goes, but try to be as specific as possible and remember to write down what kinds of feelings of gratitude each event inspired.

2. **Gratitude journal.** If you're more the narrative type, writing down a mini story of something great that happened in your week or in your life can solidify your feelings and add to the record of things you're thankful for. Some people write in their gratitude journal right before bed to help them wind down, reflect, and leave them on a positive note for the day. Or you can start your day with a few thankful things, because even if the day looks dreary, you can always write down "am still alive" and "coffee" and "did not stab anyone in last twenty-four hours" on your list.

3. **Meditate.** Practicing mindfulness meditation helps you ground yourself in the present moment. You can use this time to get your gratitude juices flowing by concentrating on things in the moment that bring you joy, like a nice-smelling candle or the warmth of the sun or the softness of your yoga pants.

4. **Write thank-you notes.** Writing a thank-you note is the ultimate kill-two-birds-with-one-stone move in your gratitude arsenal. Sitting down to reflect over a note nurtures your own feelings of thankfulness and gives you another reason

74

to tell a special someone why you love them so fucking much that you could just squeeze the crap out of 'em. Try sending one out once a month, and don't forget to include yourself on your mile-long mailing list.

5. **Choose a gratitude charm.** The two major barriers between you and your most blessed self are bad memory and low mindful awareness (basically, you forget to be grateful, or you fall out of touch with your thoughts and feelings). You can create visual cues to remind you to pause and admire your good fortune. Your "gratitude charm" could be a literal charm you wear, an art print on your wall (cut out the one on page 136 of this book!), or even another person (like that gorgeous vixen in your mirror).

75

#23 Time to Check That Fake ID

You know what's under so much of the misguided shit we do? Fear. Fear that we're not enough. Fear that we're not loved. Fear that we'll be abandoned. And that fear, like the sick shape-shifter it is, comes out in all kinds of un-fun forms: shame, anger, sadness, anxiety. Definitely anxiety. Fuck anxiety. We're sick of that dude.

You know that feeling when, as a teenager, you were in the checkout line with your gallon of horseshit vodka and you handed over your friend's fake ID? And you were super nervous for those few seconds as the cashier checked the photo, then checked you, then checked the photo again, and you knew you looked nothing like the photo?

That's kind of what happens to us in real life all the time. People are constantly slapping our photos on the ID cards they make for us. One ID card might say, "Obedient, Responsible Daughter." Another might say, "The Fun, Sparkly One." Another might say, "Head-Down, Hard Worker." And most of the time, we're carrying all those IDs around, playing into those roles, letting other people decide our identities.

But here's where shit gets busted. None of those IDs are the real you. They're all fake IDs. False identities given to us by the sometimes-well-meaning, sometimes-douche-y people in our lives. And under all those stacks of identities is the True You. And . . . sing it loud . . . Trueeeee Youuuuu is BEST YOU. True You is loved. And good enough. And never alone. Because True You's got you.

But the moment we feel a flash of fear is when people look at us, look at the fake ID they're holding, then look at us again, and they don't think we're looking like or acting like that person anymore. They're holding tight to that fixed-in-plastic idea of who we are, but me and you, sweetie pie? We are growing.

And growing means spending more time connected to True You—that accepting, open, curious, and compassionate self that comes out when you feel super centered—and less time playing out those fake ID roles. But to stop kowtowing to the judge-y cashiers in our lives, we've got to spot and name the fake IDs that we're holding on to.

NAME THE FAKE IDS

In the spaces below, list the different identities you've held at different times, with different people, and in different circumstances throughout your life. We're not here to judge those IDs (hey, they helped us do what we had to do at the time!), but we want to see them clearly so that the next time we're feeling pressured to play that part, we can spot the perpetrator and nab her before she can steal the spotlight from True You. True You is here to shine, for good.

_____

_____

_____

#24 I-N-D-E-P-E...
Just Ask for Help Already

When people look up the definition of "strong independent woman," they find a picture of you, hands on hips, hair blowing in the wind. You are absolutely a self-sufficient baddie all day every day . . . until anxiety busts down the door, wrestles you into a chokehold, and kicks you in the emotional crotch. And even then, no one will catch you calling for help because you are FIERCE.

Look, we get it. We, too, would rather hand-write our taxes, carry ten grocery bags in one hand, and unjam the shitty copying machine all at the same time than ask for assistance once. We totally support that lifestyle, but psychologists? Yeah, not so much. Our sisters in science have put their PhDs to work and have concluded the unthinkable: the more you identify your needs and ask for help, the better your psychological health will be. (Also, groundbreaking scientific discovery: pop songs are not real life. Ugh, right?)

Studies show that simply asking for help from time to time gives us a greater sense of security in our relationships and greater freedom to act. In other words, knowing what you need and how to get support creates stability. If stating "knee-ds" and requesting "hell-puh" is a foreign language to you, or if you're just a little rusty, we came prepared with this Communication Crash Course.

LISTEN TO YOUR BODY

Are your stress senses tingling? Body scan, body scan, body scan. This is your first line of defense when you feel like something is off. Put everything on pause and take thirty seconds to check in with yourself. Notice both your physical state (hunger, thirst, energy level) and your mental state (worried, nervous, distracted). Figuring out what you need begins with recognizing how you're doing in the present moment.

CREATE A "NEEDS INVENTORY" LIST

Once you know how you feel, think about the need that feeling is coming from. You might be feeling tense after sitting hunched at your desk for hours and could use a short walk, which just happens to go by your favorite coffee shop. Or maybe you're totally over someone's bullshit, and you might need to draw another mean doodle of them and yell at it. Whatever the situation is, make a list of all your emotions and then write down their corresponding needs.

ASK YOURSELF FOR HELP

Your first (and sometimes your best) resource is you. Asking yourself for help isn't a cop-out—it's about allowing yourself to fulfil your need. So just like you would complete an important work assignment, actually follow through on that shit. Give yourself time for that manicure, take a day off for you, and treat yourself to that motherfuckin' cupcake because sometimes—You. Really. Do. NEED. IT.

ASK OTHERS FOR HELP

Sometimes, meeting a need means meeting with another human being. (I know, gross.) When regular communication is a struggle, admitting that you need help with something can be even more cringy. At times like that, try one of these phrases to rip off the bandage and get the healing and help you need.

- "I've been feeling X, and I could really use some Y."
- "X has been weighing me down lately. I trust you and your opinion, so I want to know what you think I could do next."
- "I appreciate your time and effort, and I could use some advice about X."
- "Can you help me with X? I think it would help me resolve Y emotions."
- "I've tried doing X, Y, and Z, but I'm still having a hard time. Do you think you can help me figure out something else?"

An Anytime Brain Dump

Have you been ruminating about the same thing for days, picking open a wound that's only getting more bleed-y? It's time to dump those thoughts out of your brain so you can ball 'em up and throw 'em out. Countless studies have shown that journaling can help clarify your thoughts, reduce stress, and solve problems more effectively, all by the simple magic of turning thoughts into writing. And despite the hype, you don't need an Instagrammable journal, or even a journal at all, to dump out those getting-you-nowhere thoughts. Start with the blank space below, but anytime you feel the same train of thought, pull up at Misery Station, open a note-taking app on your phone, a blank text document, or even a blank email, and Let. That. Shit. Go.

#26 The UGHs and YAYs of the Day

Have you ever been having the most perfect of perfect days, killing presentations, crushing your to-do list, actually choosing kale over fries, when all of a sudden you freeze? You hear something annoyingly familiar in the distance, something too heinous to ignore. Is that Boss Battle music? The Jaws theme song? No, it's far worse than you thought . . . it's the unmistakable beating drums of your mortal enemy, the Anxiety Trigger. AagggGGHHHhhh!

A "trigger" is a person, place, event, or thing that causes a sucky feeling or crappy reaction. Like a toot after a Chipotle burrito bowl, the anxiety trigger is dangerous because it is silent, it is deadly, and it will blindside your partner right before bed (sorry, babe!). It probably seems obvious, but the best way to deal with gassy bellies and anxious feelings is to avoid the trigger as much as possible in the first place. Swerving around triggers is like avoiding awkward interactions at family get-togethers—you have to know exactly who to look out for and be ready to dodge and deflect at a moment's notice.

Keeping a list of good and bad moments for a few days is a common way to identify anxiety triggers. Feeling like the greatest badass to have ever walked the earth? Or maybe you want to shift into cocoon mode and hibernate for several long winters? Either is okay, but write it down and consider these questions.

FIVE QS TO ASK WHEN YOU GET THE FEELS

1. What happened, where were you, and when did it take place?

2. When did this feeling start?

3. Who was involved?

4. What led up to the event?

5. How does this experience compare to the last time you felt this way?

Pinpointing exact triggers not only helps you avoid them, but it also empowers you to tackle your triggers head-on. Once you understand how, when, and where your foe will strike, you can start formulating coping skills to send those demons back to the stupid pit they crawled out of. Those coping tools can be soothers, which are basically like pacifiers for babies and give you a hit of comfort and safety, or longer-term coping tools like a regular therapy session (see page 57 for advice on finding the therapist of your dreams), or they can be as simple as a five-minute grounding exercise like palming your eyes (see page 28).

Figuring out which coping tool works best for each trigger takes trial and error, but just knowing you have a whole menu of coping tools, soothing exercises, and other feel-good strategies in your back pocket at any time can help make the next anxiety attack a little less, well, anxious.

#27 Extremely Unambitious Goals

In today's installment of *The Brain is an ACTUAL Douchebag*, we find out that your brain naturally hates goal setting. Your noggin is wired to love routine, and—guess what—trying something new takes away your brain's security blanket and triggers a MASSIVE mental temper tantrum, commonly known as feeling fucking overwhelmed.

Using tiny goals in this giant-ass mess is like giving candy to our metaphorical baby brain. Each time you complete a tiny goal, like making the bed or doing a facemask (yes, self-care will always count), your brain gets a little dose of dopamine to celebrate your accomplishment and boost your overall mood. But wait, it gets better. The more you set and achieve tiny goals, the more your brain gets used to seeing that you can tackle that thing, and you'll build up confidence to take on bigger challenges.

But even once you're feeling up for medium- or big-sized challenges, make yourself limit your Big To-Dos for the day to just three things. Picking only three must-do goals a day helps clarify your priorities and make sure you get the most important things done. And the other stuff you might get to? That's the cream-cheese icing on your delicious, unicorn-sprinkle-covered cupcake.

HOW TO SET GOALS THAT WON'T CRUSH YOU INTO THE GROUND

1. Take time to reflect on realistic goals. Start with a brain dump and write down everything you want to do that day. Then, go through the list and ask yourself, "Can I realistically do this with the time, endurance, and emotional energy I have today?" If you get the slightest inkling of "no," then dump some crap into the "maybe later" pile. Trust me, it can wait a hot second. Once you have your collection of goals for the day, make sure you choose three as your must-dos. If nothing else gets done today, at least you'll have gotten these three important things done.

2. Be specific and concrete. "I'm going to eat healthy today" is a goal, buuut it's not a wildly helpful one. Like, what does "healthy" mean? Vegetables are healthy, but maybe pizza is healthy for our mental health, right, right? To avoid these kinds of gray, pizza-filled areas, try to pick goals that are detailed and doable. If we're talking food, try something like, "I'm going to eat a bowl of strawberries with my breakfast." This goal is both specific and concrete because it says exactly what you're going to do (chomp that fruit) and when you're going to do it (during breakfast). Try weaseling your way out of that one.

3. Break down a big goal into tiny goals. The hardest part of accomplishing a big goal is getting there (I know, duh), so make a road map that specifies each tiny step between point A and point B. Writing out every step prepares you for success, because you've already looked into your crystal ball and envisioned how you're going to get there. Yeah, you've basically seen the future, and Sabrina is shook.

4. Anticipate the obstacles. Reaching your goals can be a lot like a sport—you might have a winning game plan, but you never know when some asshole will kick you in the shins and throw off your game. Although you can't predict everything, it can help to try to guess at what obstacles might come up and address those things before they come so you can—double win—minimize that anxiety kick-to-the-shins when they strike!

5. Set a time frame but stay flexible. Any serial procrastinator is already intimately aware of the dangers of the Indefinite Deadline. A goal without a timeline is like a vacation without travel dates. It's a great idea, but you don't know when (or if) it's going to happen. And fuck, you could use a vacation. So saying, "I'll go for a jog at 6:30 a.m. for twenty minutes," packs way more punch than, "I'll exercise after work." And it's okay to start later or adjust your plan because life fucking happens. We're just proud of you for still being here!

I am
free.

#28 Take the Compliment, You Beautiful Bitch!

Pop the champagne, put on the party hats, and call up those dancers, because we're celebrating you right now! Why? Because you chose to flip to this page and focus on you today. That's a win in our book (that's a book pun—get it?!).

Compliments and celebrations do more than just boost our egos—they light up our brains like the Fourth of July. To your brain, hearing sincere praise is just as exciting as getting a fat check, and it wants MORE. Your noggin immediately starts pumping out dopamine as a reward that encourages you to do that shit again! So, can accepting praise and applauding wins be a little addictive? Oh, 100 percent, but that's the point. Dopamine is also tied to motivation, positivity, and focus, so it actually enhances both our mood and overall performance. Some people might call this Doping Lite, but we prefer to call it working with what we've got.

But even though our brain craves all that approval, it can still be awkward as hell to actually receive it, like, verbally, from another human. Especially if it's in public. Sometimes praise pulls up that "DEFLECT, DEFLECT" impulse, and women especially tend to dodge and redirect compliments, even when we so fully deserve them (which is 100 percent of the time, just so you know.) But you don't always have to go snail mode and hide in your shell once people see how glowingly wonderful you are. We're here to change our ways and shed our old habits (new shell, new bitch, as we like to say). This is our advice for gracefully receiving compliments and basking in your positive moments.

- **Keep it short; keep it classy; say, "Thank you."** This simple response is short, sweet, and powerful. It shows that you're both grateful and humble, which is one hell of a combo meal. If you want to add a little bit of original spice, try throwing in a "That's so kind of you" or maybe even an "I appreciate that."
- **"Thank you" is enough.** Graciously accepting the praise with a simple "thanks" is both the natural and the ideal end to the exchange. There's no need to undermine the praise with a "Oh, it's nothing!" or to enter some kind of compliment competition. You earned that nice comment, so take it and keep killing it.
- **Spread the love.** Everyone loves being appreciated, so give credit where credit is due. Acknowledging anyone who helped you is another gracious way to accept praise, and it gives you more people to celebrate with. But don't use this as a deflection tactic—if it was really you who knocked that project out of the park, don't give Mansplaining Matt from Marketing unearned credit.
- **Watch your body language.** Extra attention makes many of us nervous, so try to keep your body language relaxed and resist the urge to cross your arms. Enjoy the moment and engage with the other person by maintaining eye contact and being your friendly self.
- **Acknowledge your own hard work.** No one knows just how hard you worked more than you do. Every accomplishment is the product of lots of tiny efforts, so take time to congratulate yourself for each of those small wins.
- **Tell people about your success.** The only person who will be happier about your success than you will be your friends and family. They can celebrate with you, dispense the high-fives, buy the margaritas, and then bring up your shining moment next time you're having a dark day.

How to Forgive Someone You Want to Slap

Do you ever say, "It's okay," when it's obviously NOT okay and you want to throat-punch a bitch? Or do you simmer and stew and still have a steaming hot vendetta against the boy who pushed you in third grade? Congratulations! You don't know how to forgive. But we forgive you for that. Because, really, almost no one knows how to do it all the time. Forgiveness, like apologizing, is a lost art, and the sucker punch of it all is that if you struggle to apologize to and forgive others, you'll be SOL to really forgive yourself, too.

But why should you let something go when you've been Wronged? Or why should you not spit out that "It's cool" that you don't really mean, just to dispel a conflict? Well, it's like swiping concealer over a volcano-sized zit. It pushes the problem back temporarily, but it always doubles back to clog all your other pores, trigger a full-on lava spew, and maybe even leave a literal scar. And tons of studies show that true forgiveness boosts empathy, lowers stress, and increases your Angel Quotient by up to 23 percent. One research team found that holding onto feelings of being wronged puts literal stress on your heart and tension in your face.

With all this evidence, choosing forgiveness seems like the obvious choice, but getting to real, deep, meaningful forgiveness is not as easy as just wanting it. This road will definitely have its bumps, and you may have to take it in chunks. (Breaks allowed for slapping a pillow so you don't slap the forgivee.) And while forgiving someone else is hard, forgiving yourself can be even harder, so we've broken down both situations below.

HOW TO FORGIVE OTHERS

People suck, it's true. But ruminating on their mistakes hurts you more than it hurts them, and that's some cruel karmic bullshit. Here are some things to remember while digging deep into your kindness reserves and resisting the urge to deck the nearest idiot.

Let out all the anger energy.

Do what you need to do to let that anger energy go. Like, really, if it's legal, do it. Punch all the pillows. Go to a kickboxing class. Find somewhere to scream as loud as you can. Write that passive-aggressive email, print it out, admire your writing finesse, and finally burn it to a crisp. Anger is really exhausting, and wouldn't you rather be eating ice cream with a side of murder documentary instead?

Focus on compassion and empathy.

Try to put yourself in their shoes. Don't make excuses for them but imagine the struggles that may have motivated them. Even though, yes, it can be cathartic to dwell on how much people suck, the more nuanced truth is that no person is all good or all bad. And the hurtful choices other people make reflect their own insecurities and hurts, not yours. It's cheesy but true: hurt people hurt people.

Forgiveness breaks the cycle of hurt.

Carrying hurt feelings drags down your mood, ups your stress, and sours your overall vibe. It also makes you more likely to lash out and do things you'll have to apologize for later. You have the power to put your foot down and decide that the cycle ends here.

HOW TO FORGIVE YOURSELF

Letting yourself off the hook is about more than putting things behind you. It's a critical opportunity to resolve a personal struggle and come away stronger. Going through the four Rs of self-forgiveness can help get you there.

Responsibility

You fucked up, and it's time to own up to it. No excuses. No rationalizing. Just take responsibility. This is the hardest step, but you control how drawn out it'll be.

Remorse

This is when negative emotions, like shame and guilt, come in to throw you a pity party. These emotions are a two-sided coin, and what you do with them is SUPER IMPORTANT. Unresolved guilt can worsen your anxiety and can lead to angry or addictive behavior. Or they can be proof that you are a good person who can feel the difference between right and wrong. They can be a jumping-off point to better choices.

Restoration

Try to make amends. It's easier to cut yourself a break when you know that you did everything in your power to make up for your fuck-up.

Renewal

In the words of an ex-childhood star: Everybody makes mistakes; everybody has those days. After learning from your mistake, it's time to check in with your self-esteem. Now's the time to remind yourself that you're a human who makes mistakes and a bomb-ass bitch who deserves loads of self-love.

When Duct Tape Doesn't Do It

So, you know that dad who uses duct tape to fix everything? Flat bike tire? Duct tape. Leak in your water gun? Duct tape. Broken coffee cup? Superglue . . . with a little duct tape just to be sure.

Well, we're all one Y chromosome and a few kids short of being that dad. Whenever any crap happens, we will try to use the easiest solution to patch up the problem 100 percent of the time. And there is nothing wrong with using a bandage after a fall instead of going to the doctor . . . until you realize that some little scrapes go much deeper and are full-on fractures.

Basically, dealing with anxiety can be the same way. Sometimes—big emphasis on "sometimes"—you can get away with treating the issue at surface level. So, imagine you're in a hot room. You can cool off by taking off a jacket, but that doesn't do anything about the actual problem. The room is still hot as hell! Tackling either a stuffy room or stifling anxiety takes both short-term fixes (stripping off a jacket, Magic Mike–style) and long-term solutions (turning up that motherfuckin' AC or bustin' out of that room altogether). A patch can be as easy as a deep-breathing exercise or a short jog, but sometimes you'll want to go deeper and figure out what you're really stressing about, under all the panic.

An easy way to do this is to first identify the underlying need and then to redirect by finding a different way to meet that need. Here's how that can play out:

SCENARIO #1

The Anxiety
I feel nervous and nauseated when I have to give a presentation.

The Underlying Need
I have a healthy, normal need to feel secure and accepted, but I'm worried that people will notice my crooked teeth when I talk and judge me.

Redirection
I will accept this insecurity and start exploring ways to boost my self-image and feel secure regardless of my appearance.

SCENARIO #2

The Anxiety
My room must be in perfect order, or I can't relax.

Underlying Need
I have a need to feel some agency over my life, but right now my parents are going through a divorce, and I feel out of control.

Redirection
I will work to meet my need for agency by initiating more conversations with my parents, working through my feelings in therapy, or journaling to process through my emotions.

SCENARIO #3

The Anxiety

I'm stressed because I'm always tired and I can't concentrate.

Underlying Need

My body has a need for sleep, and it's telling me something important that I should listen to.

Redirection

Instead of stressing more or numbing with TV or the internet, I will make self-care a priority. I'll research ways to improve my sleep habits, or if specific worries are keeping me up at night, I'll work through those fears in therapy or by talking it out with a pal.

The connection between the anxiety and the underlying need may be clear-cut or far more abstract. That's why anxiety is more complicated and medically confusing than the plotline of *Grey's Anatomy*. To help shine a spotlight on the actual cause, try asking yourself these three questions:

1. How long have I felt this way?

2. What has changed during the last three months? What's happened over the past six months or year?

3. Have I felt like this before, but in a different situation? What do those moments have in common?

Sorting through these questions while being both objective and kind to yourself can be stupidly difficult, and that's where a good therapist can be a sweet, beautiful angel sent from above. And once you know what you're really trying to get at (maybe the compulsive shoe-buying is not about shoes?!), you can redirect the energy you would have spent on blindly duct-taping shit together and get the whole shebang running a little more smoothly.

How Anxiety Works

If you're reading this book, then chances are that you're our kind of person: stressed, a little clammy, and strapped into a stomach-churning anxiety rollercoaster that's looped on an endless track called Soul-Crushing Worry.

Naturally, your heart is pounding—your shirt is soaked with sweat. Your breath is getting faster and shallower, and you have to fight the sudden impulse to piss your pants. And these feelings can sucker punch you without warning at seemingly any moment. Are you feeling fucking stressed yet?

HOW ANXIETY WORKS IN YOUR BODY

Most of us can name something that causes this stress-spiking sensation (public speaking, running late, small talk with strangers, Karens asking for a manager, etc.), but how many people can explain what anxiety exactly is? While anxiety might feel like the Four Horsemen of the Apocalypse have arrived to bring utter chaos to your internal life, this emotional shit-show is actually a very organized chemical reaction designed to save your life. We know—losing sleep over an awkward exchange at a checkout counter will save me from something? It's cruel, but yes, but in a slightly different situation, that feeling could help you survive, and here's why.

Like most living creatures, we have a system of instinctual reactions that helps us navigate potentially dangerous situations, like an angry bear or an equally vicious in-law. This system is called the fight-or-flight response, and it's activated by an environmental stressor (aka the ferocious asshole that's stressing you the fuck out). Your brain is constantly on the lookout for potential threats, and it's your amygdala that's in charge of raising the alarm whenever it spots some shady activity. Once awareness of the stressor reaches the amygdala, the brain sends the "Oh Shit, We're Gonna Die" signal through the hypothalamus, which then triggers your sympathetic nervous system, or SNS for short.

The SNS is the automatic system. It officially starts the fight-or-flight response via adrenaline production, and just like a heartless robot, the SNS is ruthlessly good at its job. At this point, you're probably noticing your quickened heartbeat, muscle tightness, rapid breathing, increased sweating, and more unsettling sensations. Scientifically speaking, you've entered Balls to the Wall Survival Mode. Your body is coursing with extra oxygen, and your increased heartbeat is pushing that oxygenated blood out to your limbs and preparing you for action. As crazy complex as this process seems so far, experiencing anxiety only gets more complicated in its next phase, known as "Having Emotions."

HOW ANXIETY FEELS

Everything described so far is your body's physical response to chemical signals, but the way you feel about your physical reaction is another beast entirely. The emotions we feel from our fight-or-flight response will be one of three options: fear, anxiety, or panic (the options couldn't be better, right?). But wait, aren't these all different words for the same shit? You would think so, but no! Just like snowflakes with an affinity for destroying your happiness, they're all special in their own way.

Fear is the emotion we have when facing a real threat in our IRL environment, like when we see a small, skittering creature that could be a dangerous spider. It's caused by a real and present danger, so it goes away as soon as the threat is gone.

Anxiety is what fear would be if it lost its sense of reality (and its common-fucking-sense, to be honest). It's our emotional response to an unrealistic threat that is unlikely to ever happen. Feeling anxious would be like refusing to go into anybody's house, ever, because there's a chance there's a spider in there. Anxiety is about being motivated or demotivated by the IDEA of a threat rather than the real deal. Anxiety is the fear of what could be instead of what actually is, and this is what makes it so maddeningly difficult to shake. And panic is basically anxiety on steroids. It's an intense rush of anxious feelings that usually lasts for ten to twenty minutes.

Although they may feel like just a giant pain in the ass, these emotions push us to avoid things that could harm us. As cavemen, feeling anxiety after recognizing a predator's paw print was really important for, you know, staying alive? This instinctive emotion, which helped our ancestors avoid man-eating beasts, persists in humans to this day . . . but unfortunately, our amygdala did not evolve like our bodies. Despite how fucking smart we are today, the amygdala thinks that making small talk with your ex in the checkout line is just as life-endangering as a mountain lion roaring in your face. (Mountain lion's got better breath, though.)

WHAT WE CAN DO

So how the hell can we control an instinctual reaction? Well, we can't control the response itself, but we CAN control what happens around it. Noticing what stressors trigger your inner alarms and then learning ways to curb that response as quickly as possible will give you the upper hand in the struggle with your amygdala for emotional control. Finding resources and exercises that break the anxiety spiral and physically calm your body can bring you back to the state of homeostasis that you deserve.

Unlike the fight-or-flight response, the battle against your anxiety takes a fuck-ton of conscious effort. Your history of coping with anxiety may be long and well-established, or it might just be getting started, but wherever you are in the process, this book is here to offer at least a few more tools for your personal arsenal.

Part two

build + flex your anti-anxiety powers on the daily

For most of us, the struggle with anxiety is real and daily. But we can flex up on that asshole by layering in healthy habits and self-care to stay grounded and centered when anxiety wants to shove us off-balance.

Chapter Three will offer up a big dose of grace in the form of the shortest, most wildly manageable self-care regimen ever. Because feeling bad about your lifestyle has never made anyone less anxious.

In Chapter Four, you'll learn to practice some totally cheesy and super-worth-it self-love, plus hear some hard-hitting TRUTHS for shitty situations. This chapter will show you, day-by-day, how to build love and tenderness for yourself, so you can be stronger and more resilient in the face of all the terrifying crap in the world.

In Chapter Five, we'll chill the fuck OUT. You'll find the good stuff like color-by-numbers pages (no more overthinking your color choices), empowering word searches (so you literally find "self-respect"), mantra calligraphy (crappy handwriting encouraged), and soothing labyrinths (no decisions required!).

Together, these activities can interrupt the negative patterns in our bodies and brains and show us that we can, in fact, soothe our sweet, damn adorable selves.

CHAPTE

do these eight things every

R THREE

day—yOu DeSeRvE iT!

#32 Breathe, Then Breathe Again

We all have moments when we just can't, right? Like, your daily ration of Fucks-To-Give wasn't delivered, and now you literally couldn't spare a fuck even if you wanted to. When I feel like this, I'll be doing one of four things: crying, resenting, anxiety-spiraling, or people-punching. To use the technical term, I feel like "C.R.A.P." Maybe you've felt it, too?

Whether it's one sucky moment or a full-blown retreat to the blanket-cocoon, it's totally valid to feel like shit sometimes and to do the bare minimum. During these kinds of C.R.A.P.-fests, using the energy you have wisely is priority number one. So, if you do nothing else today, take a quality breath. To your body, low oxygen is like a hairspray shortage at a dance recital—it's the beginning of a glitter-coated meltdown.

But it only takes one belly-expanding breath to pull in loads of air that will replenish the blood's oxygen supply. Restoring blood oxygen levels is the code green message that tells your body to pump the breaks, slow your heart rate, and relax your muscles. And that little signal can be the first step to rescuing a categorically C.R.A.P. day.

So, take that breath and maybe take another (there's no such thing as "greedy" when the air is free, right?). If you want to deepen your breath, try a simple breathing technique like this one.

4-7-8 BREATHING

1. Put your tongue behind your front teeth. Then, press your tongue against the top of your gums.

2. Exhale all of your breath through your mouth. You'll hear a soft whooshing sound.

3. Close your mouth, and breathe in through your nose while counting to four.

4. Hold the breath for seven counts.

5. Breathe out through your mouth for eight counts.

6. Inhale and repeat the 4-7-8 breathing cycle three more times.

Breathing exercises like this can be your oasis in the middle of a desert of bullshit. They're here to be your literal breath of fresh air whenever and wherever you need it. So, here are a few times throughout your day when you can flick on the "ON AIR" light and shut the mental door to any interruptions.

- While waiting in line at the store
- Sitting on the toilet
- Sitting at your desk or on the couch
- Waiting for the microwave to beep
- Idling at a red light
- Watching commercial breaks
- Sipping a hot drink
- Listening to music
- Pumping gas
- Eating a snack
- Doing your hair
- Touching up your makeup
- Doing laundry
- Winding down for bed

#33 Listen to Your Body

Shhhhhh, listen. Do you hear that? No, it's not the satisfying crackle of flames engulfing your ex's comic book collection. It's the screams of your anxious body and its long-ignored cries for help! Aches and pains, fatigue and tummy problems—all of these are bodily Bat-Signals sent out to warn you about an ongoing attack from your mortal enemy: Anxietus von Hell-Bringer (*distant thunderclap*).

When Anxiety goes on a villainous rampage, it cranks up the cortisol—aka your stress chemicals—into one thousand-billion-cajillion percent overdrive (approximately). And just like in a movie fight scene, your body takes a beating left and right, with an acne breakout here and a catastrophic headache there.

So, what do most of us do when our body throws up a distress sign? We straight-up ignore that shit. That nervous pee? It can wait. Your restless knee? No one will notice the vibrating floor . . . is what you tell yourself. And your extra sweaty pits? Well, that's just the weather. Even though it's winter.

But where does this it's-normal-to-overlook-our-physical-needs bullshit even come from? Your friendly neighborhood therapist would tell you that people will deny their body as a sign of physical control. For example, "only kids need snacks" translates to "ignoring hunger pangs proves that you're exerting willpower over the body like an adult."

Well, we're calling bullshit on shitting on our bodies right now. And instead, we're going to start loving on this beautiful cocoon we wear every day by dialing into our body's small requests. Tackling these mini-needs as they appear reminds your body that things are okay—that you are okay.

SIGNALS FROM YOUR BODY

- Fidgeting and restlessness
- Clammy hands
- Rapid heartbeat or chest tightness
- Nail biting
- Stomachache
- Teeth grinding
- Headaches
- Curling hands and feet
- Picking the skin
- Tense muscles
- Exhaustion
- Fluctuating appetite
- Breakouts and other skin problems

REMEDIES

- Five-minute stretch break
- Deep breathing exercise
- Snack on some fruits and veggies
- Drink a soothing tea
- Take a bathroom break
- Chew gum and focus on the flavor
- Palm your eyes
- Give yourself a hand massage
- Take a hot bath or shower
- Lay down for a twenty-minute power nap
- Replace large meals with several small ones
- More self-care sessions, overall!

 # Pee and Poop When You Need To

Anxiety is like a punch to the "activate" button on your fight-or-flight system. This instinctive "OMG-I'm-about-to-die" reaction prepares you to defend yourself from any threat, like a ferocious bear or that sales report due next Thursday. It accelerates your heartbeat, quickens your breath, and . . . makes you want to pee your pants?

Yes! That sudden pre-presentation pee panic is a nerve-wracking sign that your sympathetic nervous system is working great (lucky you!). Although it seems like a cruel design flaw, the bladder and the digestive tract are best friends with the fight-or-flight response and very sensitive to it because of that. Like, we're talking Chihuahua-that-needs-a-security-blanket levels of skittish. So, when you're at ease, your pee and poo centers slowly fill up and send messages to the brain, saying, "Things are all good!" or "Yeah, it's literally kinda crappy down here." But when the Panic Party rolls through, all of your muscles tense up. And we mean all of them.

But no need to get anxious about your bathroom habits (because the power of suggestion is real). There are just three easy steps to answering the question: To Pee or Not To Pee?

CHECK IN WITH YOUR BODY

No one knows your body's natural pee and poop cycle better than you, so if you sense that something's out of whack, suss that shit out. Take a moment and ask, "Should I really need to go already, or am I reacting to something else?"

DON'T DELAY THE DEFECATION

Going when you need to go is defense number one (and number two *wink*). We may not realize it, but a lot of us put off a trip to the bathroom until it's "convenient," like after you finish an email or whenever an episode is over. But here's the thing: peeing and pooping is not a chore that you can delay. It's an ESSENTIAL BODILY FUNCTION. So, if you need to go, take five minutes and go! It will take pressure off your organs and your mind.

BREATHE THROUGH THE STRESS URGE

If you know that this is a stress pee and not a legit pee, try controlling your fight-or-flight response. Doctors often recommend going through a deep-breathing routine to soothe the sympathetic nervous system and turn down the stress dial. Or, if you know that a stress bomb is incoming, prepare twenty minutes ahead with a grounding exercise. Your mind and your bowels will thank you.

So, now that you know that any time can be tinkle time, maybe you want to upgrade your toilet's three-star ambiance to a five-star resort experience that you'll never want to leave? Don't worry—we have ideas.

- Candles and potpourri
- Toilet spray (for before you go)
- The finest three-ply toilet paper
- Wipe dispenser
- Hand soap with essential oils
- Matching hand and bath towels
- Toilet squatty stool
- The plushest bathmat
- Motion sensor trash can
- Multicolor lights that go *in* your toilet

109

#35 Sleep, Or At Least Put Yourself to Bed

Have you ever looked at the clock and thought, "If I fall asleep in five minutes, then I can get six hours, forty-three minutes, and seventeen seconds of sleep"? But plot twist: your anxiety monster rolls out from under the bed, gobbles up your brain, and churns out a highlight reel of every anxiety-producing thought known to womankind.

Countless studies have proven that sleep (or even just a short rest) is the key to turning the tide in our Battle with Anxiety. But sometimes anxiety about *not* being able to fall asleep can make it even *harder* to fall asleep, because life's a cruel bitch like that. And while you might not be able to hit that seven to nine hours every single night, you can at least try these tweaks to set yourself up for some successful stomping of your under-the-bed anxiety monster.

BLOCK BLUE LIGHT

Blue light is a section of the light spectrum that tells our brain "Hey! It's daytime—don't sleep!" It literally controls our body's melatonin production by reducing the hormone that helps us feel all relaxed and snoozy. We're naturally exposed to it during the day in the form of sunlight, but we also get a blast of the blue from electronic devices like, you know, the phone you probably stare at every night before bed. Ideally, you should avoid blue light two hours before sleeping. Realistically, try to cut back on your evening screen time and use apps (like f.lux) or device settings to reduce blue light.

CUT THE CAFFEINE

A late night latte run is a blast, especially six hours later when we can't get to sleep to save our lives. Sleep experts recommend cutting caffeinated drinks at least six hours before going to sleep (caffeine can stay in your bloodstream for eight hours!). But if ya gotta have one, go for the decaf option during your evening café run.

EMBRACE TUB TIME

In some countries, a nightly bath is a cultural staple. And some scientists think they're onto something. One study found that taking a warm bath, shower, or even a foot soak within ninety minutes of going to bed improved overall sleep quality. So basically, your bubble bath isn't a "luxury." It's an essential part of your health care.

SET THE MOOD

The bedroom is your sleep sanctuary, and it should be spruced up like the sacred little den of safety it is. Studies show that lighting, noise, smell, temperature, and even furniture can make the difference between a shitty snooze and a top-tier hibernation fest. An optimal sleep cave will be chilly, quiet, and darker than the 6 p.m. coffee you recently gave up (RIP old friend).

CHOOSE A WIND-DOWN ACTIVITY

Your pre-sleep routine is your chance to let go of the day. But going from sixty to zero can be hard (especially after a shitty day). So many sleep enthusiasts start prepping for quality Z's by doing activities that calm their thoughts, like journaling, reading, meditation, puzzles, word searches, or sudokus. Whatever you choose, the goal is to dump your day and its baggage at the door and focus on you.

111

#36 Move for Ten Minutes

A lot of us have two speeds and two speeds only: 1) running in a lathered-up panic, or 2) barely making it from the couch to the fridge. And just like your love of cheese and your lactose intolerance, neither can happily exist at the same time.

And we all know which lifestyle is obviously better: couch potato with a side of cheese, please. But weirdly enough, research says otherwise? Annoyingly, studies on mental health and exercise have found that regular physical activity may be just as effective at managing anxiety as prescription medications. One study concluded that people who did strenuous exercise regularly (like running or biking) lowered their chances of developing anxiety or depression by—get this—a whopping 25-motherfuckin'-percent. With a discount that deep, we'll take your entire stock. (And we'll still take that cheese, thanks.)

Research also tells us that you can kick-start endorphin production with less than ten minutes of aerobic exercise, more commonly known by its stage name, Cardi O. Activities like walking (at the mall), swimming (in a hot tub), and hiking (back upstairs to your bed) can all count toward your daily cardio goal. So don't be ashamed to be extremely unambitious here. Fuck getting up at 5 a.m. to slog to a sweaty-ass gym. Instead, decide you'll do just ten minutes a day of walking, yoga, gardening, body weight exercises, or anything else you don't hate. And if you need a quickie stretch routine, turn to page 39 for "The Easiest Five Minutes of Yoga Ever." (Spoiler alert: It's like regular exercise, but a lot fucking easier and comes with a side of blankets. You're welcome.)

For more ways to move one more inch off the couch, here's a starter list of stuff to try. Just remember: it doesn't have to be "fitness" (whatever the fuck that really is) for it to be a healthy way to move your body.

MIX-AND-MATCH MOVEMENT ACTIVITIES

- Dancing
- Jumping rope
- Gardening
- Hiking
- Power-walking
- Swimming
- Kickboxing
- Biking
- Jogging
- Trampoline-ing
- Sailing or rowing
- Skateboarding
- Hula-hooping
- Jumping jacks
- Stair climbing
- Roller skating

#37 Drink Some Water

Do you hate water? Like, not interested; it tastes like nothing; you're not even thirsty; straight-up fuck-that-shit? Well, we have something to tell you. Water is ESSENTIAL FOR LIFE. You will die without it. Your brain will almost start wilting—dehydration saps your brain's energy, impedes serotonin (happy chemical) production, and increases stress on your body. Also, your skin will shrivel up like a prune (less scientifically validated but still SCARY, right?). So stop parching yourself, and start watering yourself like the beautiful fiddle-leaf fig you are.

Here's how to start doing this thing you might not want to do. Start small. Sip, sip, sip. Start with a little shot glass if you need to. Because the more you drink water, the more you will start to notice your thirst. Because if you think you're not thirsty, it's probably because you're out-of-tune with your body. You may be so perpetually parched that it's your normal. But as you start with drinking two glasses a day, then working up to three, then four and five, you may soon realize that you want to drink water because you are THIRSTY AS FUCK.

So the challenge likely won't be to stick to this habit once you get into it—the challenge will be to commit to that one tiny step toward it, then gradually build up from there. Here are a few tips for inching your way to more water a day. Take it slow with just one or two of these tips to start, and once you're doing one of these mini-habits without thinking about it, add in another. Soon, your body will start telling you when it wants water, and all you gotta do is listen to the lady. She knows her shit.

HOW TO ACTUALLY DRINK MORE WATER

1. Set a glass of water on your nightstand, and drink it as soon as you wake up. You'll instantly feel more awake.

2. Get a water bottle you love and take it everywhere with you. Just the act of carting it around—to the car, your desk, the gym, whatever—will remind you to sip from it.

3. Before you eat, pause and drink a half or whole glass of water first. You'll feel fuller sooner and digest better.

4. Add whatever kind of whacky flavors you need to make water taste like something you actually want to drink. We love True Lemon packets because they are just dehydrated lemon without weird shit in it (and it comes in lime, orange, and grapefruit!). But just go to the water aisle at the grocery store and buy whatever the hell you need to make it work.

5. Stock up on sparkling water, flavored seltzers, and any other non-soda, water-y drinks you like. Those count as water, too!

#38 Eat One Vegetable a Day

Listen. I love pizza. I live, breathe, bleed, and die pizza. I'm basically thirty extra-large pepperoni pizzas stacked inside a trench coat, pretending to be human. BUT. When I spend a whole weekend gorging on different combinations of bread, cheese, and meat, I feel extra shitty on Monday morning. And not just the usual work-sucks, bloated-and-hungover feeling. I feel anxious as fuck. Maybe you, too?

That's because: SCIENCE. Many recent studies have shown that gut bacteria can influence our moods and amplify anxiety, depression, and stress. And serotonin, which is what most antidepressants work to increase, is actually manufactured in our guts, not in our brains. So on top of the general suckiness of Monday (or whatever day is currently being a crap-fest), plus your anxious thoughts popping up like sick whack-a-mole, the actual bacteria in your stomach could be contributing to the anxiety flame war. Very rude.

While we can't control all the annoying stressors around us, or wrestle every last anxious thought to the ground, one thing we can do is pop a few veggies and fruits in our bodies to feed the nice bacteria instead of the screaming-at-the-top-of-their-lungs bugs.

One of the easiest ways to do this is to have vegetables you actually like (fuck you, eggplant) stocked in the fridge, as well as dressings that can make anything taste like, well, delicious dressings. The goal here is to get even just one vegetable or fruit into your body every day. If you can work up from there to two to three servings per day, well, you are my hero, girl.

If you're feeling prep-y, try to spend fifteen minutes on the weekend chopping a few fresh veggies or fruits for snacking, or roasting a tray or two of vegetables for dinner side dishes. If you like to cook, you can also plan and prep one or two of your favorite veggie-packed dinners that you can quickly throw together during the week. (Stir-fries, frittatas, and grain bowls will never let you down.) Because let's be real. There's literally no fucking way we're going to push ourselves to cook veggies if we've just had the worst day at work and our bodies are screaming for pizza-and-couch therapy.

Start by circling the vegetables you love most from the list below. It's easy to fall in a rut or go blank once you start writing your grocery list, so refer back to this list if you're ever feeling listless about your shiny new One Veg a Day lifestyle. Then stock up on some of your favorite sauces and dressings, choose a few veggie-packed dinners you could add to your rotation, and start noticing just how much happier your little gut bacteria friends are when you give them the good stuff.

VEGGIES + FRUITS

Lettuce	Beets
Tomatoes	Kale
Cucumber	Eggplant
Carrots	Peppers
Cauliflower	Zucchini
Broccoli	Apples
Cabbage	Bananas
Spinach	Oranges
Green Beans	Berries
Squash	Pears
Asparagus	Grapes
Brussels Sprouts	Peaches

117

DRESS IT UP

Buffalo Sauce	General Tso's
Bleu Cheese	Hummus
Ranch	Salsa
Honey Mustard	Tzatziki
Alfredo Sauce	Peanut Sauce
Queso	Wasabi Mayo
Green Goddess	Hot Honey
Barbeque Sauce	Garlic Aioli
Olive Oil and Vinegar	Hot Sauce
Pesto	Whipped Cream
Teriyaki	Peanut Butter

A FEW VEG-PACKED MEALS I ACTUALLY LIKE

_____

_____

_____

_____

_____

_____

_____

_____

_____

_____

THEY WILL NEVER TAKE MY POWER.

#39 Put Away Your Phone for Twenty Minutes

When people ask if I have significant other, I answer honestly and say, "Yes, I'm in a committed relationship with my phone." My phone and I are always by each other's side, and we're the first and last thing the other sees every day. Haters say that it won't last, but I have a little phone-shaped divot in my heart (and my hand) that says otherwise.

So, can tech and people really have a perfect partnership? Oh, hell no. Screens are VERY needy. One moment they're pestering you over a missed text, the next they're complaining about running low on energy (for the third fucking time today), and then they're being an actual pain in the neck from all the stooping to their level. It's exhausting.

Besides just wearing you the fuck out, too much screen time strains your eyes, lowers the quality of your sleep, and reduces your attention span. In fact, research shows that constantly checking our tech has made the average human attention span shorter than a goldfish's! Like, what the actual fuck.

Technology is addictive because it gives us instant satisfaction for a brief moment. But we can break free from this addictive, one-sided relationship by . . . drum roll please . . . putting the fucking phone away. Yes, it's true: less screen time is healing, and it can be a time to send some love and attention to other parts of You.

Word from our Science Squad says that as little as fifteen to twenty minutes of self-reflection (not the same thing as a selfie) a day can help foster a positive mindset, improve your emotional state, and raise your overall performance by 23 percent. But if getting all introspective and in your feels makes you want to cringe, that's okay. The real point here is to get into the habit of spending time away from all screens for at least twenty minutes a day. Once your brain isn't one endless scroll of shiny stimuli, if you start to feel a twinge of boredom and the itch to "just quickly check" your phone, turn to one of these questions instead.

CHECK IN WITH YOU INSTEAD OF THEM

1. How am I doing physically? How about mentally?
2. What do I need? How can I get it?
3. What can I do to improve my perspective?
4. Am I letting something out of my control contribute to my current stress?
5. Have I been setting and achieving reasonable goals?
6. How do I see myself? Am I staying true to that self?
7. What is something I couldn't live without? Why?
8. When was the last time I left my comfort zone or took a chance?
9. How do I fit into the greater scheme of things, and am I fulfilling my role?
10. What are my most treasured relationships? What am I doing to maintain them?

CHAPTE

truths + tending

Turn here
when shit
sucks!

ER FOUR

for shitty situations

You are beautiful.

When You Feel Stuck #40

Feeling "stuck" is basically what happens when statements such as "I should do X" or "I have to Y" take over your entire mood. We usually feel this way when we feel like life isn't going how it should and that it's because we're not doing something that we should be.

The struggle can feel so real in these moments because that's all it is—struggle. You may be pushing yourself to make changes that might not even be needed (or possible!). Next time you hear yourself uttering that perfectionistic "should," ask yourself if you even really want to. Maybe there's a different way to meet that goal (if it's even your goal and not one dropped on you by some dirtbag), or maybe you want to just click-and-drag that goal to the trash. Remember that there are literally very few things you truly should do—like not murder grannies—and everything else is OPTIONAL. As in, you can opt out. Bye, dumb expectation!

#41 When You're Worried Someone Doesn't Like You

Wanting to be liked is a good thing because it can inspire people to be more kind and caring to others. BUT it's also the sharpest of double-edged swords, and it will just as quickly cut you down with the simple threat of being disliked or abandoned.

It's okay to want to grow and to live by your own standards— like, would you want to be friends with you? But you should never pin your happiness on what some random asshat thinks about you. We all know that it's impossible to please everyone, so basing your worth on something you can't control is an unwinnable battle. The best thing you can do is spend as much time as you can with people who truly appreciate you because, at the end of the day, the people who really love you will always overshadow the couple of clowns who failed to recognize that you're a gem that sparkle-sparkles.

When You Feel Like You're a Bad Person

#42

First of all, there are no truly "bad" people—just mixed up and misguided people. So, you already have no reason to worry. Second, "feeling like a bad person" is usually just that: a feeling, not a fact. The idea that we're bad often comes from the sense that we failed to meet an expectation, like the expectation to excel or the expectation to choose frozen yogurt over ice cream (which is just cruel, tbh).

Here, we have to stop and challenge these thoughts by asking, "Why do I feel like doing X, Y, or Z makes me a bad person?" The point is to separate actual actions that caused harm from negative emotions that have grown out of proportion. Try journaling or talking to a friend or therapist if you need help sorting out what's what in this shame-y muck. This process takes time and reflection, but it also reaffirms who you really are: a thoughtful, caring, and GOOD person.

#13 When You Feel Unlovable

First off, you are SO loved. Secondly, nearly everyone feels this way sometimes. The psychopaths that run the misogynistic side of media and marketing are gunning for you to feel Less-Than so they can sell you shit. Too bad for them, because you are More-Than. More than any dumb comparison to what someone else has or is. More than what anyone thinks of you. More than even this feeling and this moment.

You are a bright, glowing ball of beautiful, shining goodness at your core. And that core—the True You that yearns for goodness and love—was put there by Whatever You Call Your Bigger Power, and so it can't ever go away. No take-backsies on that one. So even when there are some parts of you and some people in your life that obscure that light, it's still there. Always. Because you are SO loved. It's a fact.

When You Feel Unpretty

We've all gone from feeling Hawt as Fuck one minute to reaching for a paper bag as a face accessory. Scientifically called "feeling fugly," this misguided but extremely powerful emotion is often rooted in—yep, you guessed it!—shame and body insecurity. A big part of these issues stems from attention bias, meaning latching onto a small list of things and completely overlooking the rest. This would mean seeing the traits of a perfect(ly unrealistic) and highly photoshopped model and then looking for those traits in ourselves to measure our prettiness.

To correct this habit, psychologists tell us to fight fire with fucking fire and build our self-image up with pep talks in the mirror. As silly as it sounds, repeatedly identifying what makes you pretty and saying it out loud reframes your perception of beauty and redefines your standards to rightfully encompass the unparalleled goddess you are. And if you need some more fucking fire, remember that believing you are beautiful is the best way to tear down the patriarchy and let it BURN into a flaming pile of wreckage and bullshit that we won't put up with anymore.

#45 When You Feel Worthless

People who strive to achieve are driven by many positive attributes like ambition, willpower, and confidence. But on the flip side, the pressure to always perform at such a high level can create a fear of missing those self-imposed benchmarks and feeling worthless because of that.

Countering feelings of worthlessness is all about re-grounding yourself in the present rather than the future. The future is not here and—this is some weird metaphysical shit—it is never here. Only right now exists. And right now, you don't need to do jack-shit to be a good, worthy person. Try to gently remind yourself that embracing your vulnerability is a strong, self-loving thing to do, and that you are not what you do or don't do. You are you, and you are great even if you don't do even one more fucking thing for the rest of your entire life and just sit on the couch and eat chips for the next sixty years. You would still be a worthy, fucking lovely human being.

When You Feel Insignificant

Each of us is always the protagonist of our own stories, but sometimes we feel smol and not in a cute way. Constant stress can make you feel isolated from the rest of the world (no one else could possibly understand your emotions, right?). That sense of detachment can make you feel unseen and insignificant, but that's not really what you are.

This is the time to reach out to the people close to you and let yourself actually let go and soak in how much they care about you. The truth is that you are Crazy Significant to someone, even if it's the sweet little doggo staring up at you like you dropped from heaven (ya did!). Try to see yourself from their perspective, because they don't think you're TheBomb.com for nothing. And remember that it's okay to kick back and feel that you matter—it doesn't make you arrogant; it just makes you in touch with reality!

#47 When You Feel Frazzled

Being "frazzled" is the technical term for staying on the Stress Carousel for so long that the world keeps spinning days after you've gotten off the ride. That dizziness can make you feel like you're moving and thinking at a breakneck speed, so finding a way to pump the brakes is priority number one. Recenter yourself by going into mega slow-mo, and when we say "slow," we mean S . . . L . . . O . . . O . . . O . . . O . . . W.

Challenge yourself to do an everyday activity, like making coffee or putting on your shoes, so slowly that a sloth dripping in molasses could leave you in the dust. Doing things in 0.25x speed does more than make you laugh at yourself; it forces you back into a more livable speed and reminds you that "Hey, that other shit can wait."

When You Feel Lost #48

You have a lot to offer—your brains, your beauty, your excellent taste in reading material about dealing with anxiety, and so much more. But! The one thing you don't have is All The Answers because that's, say it with me now: Not. Your. Fucking. Job. Like, we have Magic Eight Balls for a reason, right?

Feeling lost or not knowing the answer right now isn't the end of the world; it's an opportunity to thoughtfully consider all of your possibilities. So, slow down and let yourself sit with the anxiety of uncertainty. It might not feel good, but it's manageable (and if it's not, you have a whole book of ways to channel it until it's carry-able right in your hands). Take stock of where you are, and instead of berating yourself to Figure It Out NOW, accept that, right now, you're just sitting with the questions, and that's okay.

#49 When You Feel Suffocated

Have you ever watched that scene in a movie where someone is stuck in a room and the walls are slowly moving in to crush them? And have you ever felt like that threat of suffocation is a little too relatable? Yeah, us too. Feeling suffocated comes from feeling trapped: trapped by an overloaded schedule, or a toxic relationship, or anything else that seems inescapable. The key word in this statement is "seems" because you always have options, no matter how much crap is hitting the fan.

If you feel like the only options in front of you are a strict this-or-that, step back and talk to a friend or your therapist, because there are always lots of options in any situation. You never have to feel suffocated, stuck, or trapped in a situation you don't want to be in, and learning to spot and make new choices is a bomb-ass way to get the fuck outta Dodge when you need to.

When You Feel Abandoned

Let's get one thing straight: feeling alone and being alone are two TOTALLY different things. That's why you can feel isolated at a packed mall yet completely content in the car by yourself. The sense of abandonment falls under the former because it's caused by other negative emotions, like feeling unwanted or discarded (both a 10 out of 10 on the Super Sucky Scale).

If you feel like this, the first thing you should do is reaffirm your relationship with the one and only YOU. You are your own soulmate, and you need to value yourself as such. So, take yourself on a date, compliment your fantastic sense of fashion, and most importantly, be kind and supportive of yourself. Remember that you can never be abandoned, because you've always got you, and you are fucking amazing.

YOU
ARE
LOVED

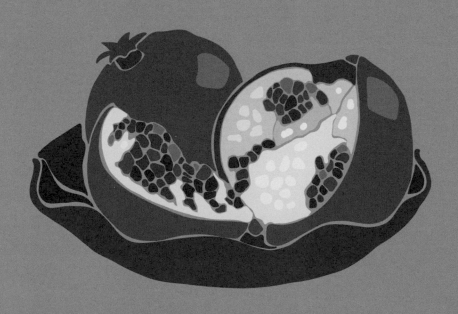

When You Can't Sleep #51

Not being able to sleep even though you're tired usually happens because something is stopping you from winding down to a peaceful state of mind. But let's be real. If you could turn your anxiety off like a light switch, you wouldn't be reading this book or lying awake at night and worrying about whether you hit "send" on that email or fever-dreamed the whole thing.

Instead, a better strategy is to develop a buffer zone between your active state and your bedtime mode. This intermediate time will be dedicated to slowing down and sloughing off the day's BS bit by bit. Try creating a routine that cuts out screen time, incorporates self-care, and includes something like journaling that lets you dump any lingering thoughts. For more advice, check out page 110 for tips for optimizing your rest.

#52 When You Feel Helpless

You know what feels nice? Being in control. Unfortunately, it's LITERALLY IMPOSSIBLE to be in control of everything. Sux, we know. But things like the weather, your neighbor's dog, and the ripeness of the avocado on your counter all have a mind of their fucking own and don't give a shit about you or your plans. And you know what? Fuck them.

Instead of feeling helpless, take a few minutes to write out a list of all of those little inconsiderate pricks that exist out of your control, cross them off, and let go of some of that shit. Trust us, they won't miss you, and you shouldn't miss them either.

When You're Mad at Yourself #53

Self-awareness is an essential part of self-growth, but left unchecked, that powerful tool can easily cross over into self-bullying and needless anger. Whereas accountability can be fed by the desire to improve or reach the best version of yourself, being mad at yourself is an unproductive space because it is fueled by negative motives like disappointment, shame, or regret. Worst of all, it blocks us from the most important step in the process of moving on: self-forgiveness.

So, when you're angry with yourself, strive to be as unconditionally forgiving as possible. Or if that's too difficult, try to imagine what you would do if your friend was in the same position (hint: you would probably forgive them instantly, so why don't you deserve the same?).

CHAPTE

a grab bag of ways

You look
like you
need a
break.

ER FIVE

to be amazing to you

#54 Treat Yourself

Imagine this: You're on your laptop, innocently surfing the web, when you're blindsided by a familiar foe—a flash-sale ad for your favorite online retailer! All of a sudden, your bank account begins to sweat, and you hear yourself unintentionally blurt out the universal mantra of shopaholics everywhere: TREAT YOURSELF.

As a regular customer at Retail Therapy, I completely support the occasional impulse buy (I gotta keep my credit card on its toes, after all). Like, do I really need a pair of asymmetrical jeans? Oh, no way in hell. But will they be total fire in my next Instagram pic? Abso-fucking-lutely.

My sisters-in-shopping know that clicking "Add to Cart" is a direct injection of serotonin to the brain. But did you know that you can also get that boost by doing healthy, kind things for yourself (and your bank account)? It's all about pausing to ask yourself, "What would feel good right now?" Is another shoulder bag *really* going to make you feel better in the long run? Or is what you really need to sit and cry, punch a pillow, journal out your thoughts, or just take a nap?

Treating yourself is an act of self-love, aka doing something for you and you only because you're MORE than worth it. So, if you're sleepy, take that nap. If your brain is about to explode with racing thoughts, give yourself the time to journal and vent that shit out. Or maybe you would kill for a cavity-inducing dessert? Great! Bake a cake, and eat it, too, as long as you're doing it from a place of self-love instead of just sugar-bombing your feels.

Need some more inspo? Then keep reading this chapter to find out more ways to make self-care and self-love your new lifestyle.

Cuddle Something #55

Have you ever felt so overwhelmed that you grab the nearest cushion and just smoosh it to your ridiculously stressed face? Great! Squeeze the shit out of that pillow, because your body needs it more than you know.

For your body, physical contact like cuddling can turn down your internal alarm system from a panicky 9 to a simmering 5.5. A little thing like hugging a pillow can be the long overdue bitch-slap to your hormones that decreases your cortisol and shoves some oxytocin (the "love" hormone) in its place.

Cuddling is connected to a crap-ton of health benefits, like a stronger immune system, better mental health, higher self-confidence, and elevated shower-singing prowess (probably). Although that last benefit isn't proven yet, the positive power of the cuddle is undeniable.

If we lost you at "physical contact," then that's okay, too! Whether you don't like germs or just don't like people (arguably the biggest germ of all, tbh), everyone has different comfort levels when it comes to touching, so knowing what you enjoy is key to a quality cuddle or satisfying squeeze.

Hug preference can range from the totally not awkward side-squeeze to an overly aggressive bearhug, and cuddling preference exists on the same broad spectrum. From major snuggle-fest to a little handholding or from a warm body to a body pillow, the way you get in your cuddle time is totally dependent on what you need to feel comforted. Whatever your style is, cuddle time is your moment to step back from the chaos and reset your hormones with a reassuring embrace.

#56 Vent

So, you know how laptops have fans that pump out all that hot-ass air? And you know how a computer has to vent the heat from its motherboard or it'll fucking melt into a pool of lava on your lap? Well, your brain is a motherboard, and your pent-up thoughts are a lethal heat tornado that needs venting now.

THREE WAYS TO VENT THAT RAGE

1. **Get physical.** Before you punch that jerk right in his smug face, listen to this: research says that you should use exercise as an outlet for that punchy energy. Physical activity, like hitting the gym, kickboxing, or even punching a pillow and screaming, lets us burn off the restlessness and tension during stressful situations. And avoid arrest.

2. **Cry your eyes out.** Crying is actually one of the most badass things that your body can do, and here's why: When you cry, you're literally *expelling motherfucking toxins from your eyeballs*. Crying triggers your brain's production of self-soothing chemicals, like oxytocin and endorphins. Even crazier, your tears also wash out stress hormones, so your eyes are an actual vent for liquefied frustration.

3. **Say it like it is.** Un-vented thoughts are like rotting leftovers in the fridge—the longer you ignore them, the worse and more toxic they get. Working through our thoughts, either out-loud, in writing, or visually, can help us pinpoint exactly what the problem is so it feels manageable instead of confusingly rage-inducing.

Sip Anything #57

Do you consume so little water that your succulent asks if you're okay? If so, now's the time to revamp your hydration game. Being well-hydrated has been proven to improve your physical health, cognition, and overall mood. And you can get there without feeling like you're drowning yourself in pure H2O and slowly dying of flavor boredom. So, when you're ready to rework your parched ways, try sipping on one of these stress-fighting drinks.

STRESS-SLAYING SIPPERS

1. **Valerian root tea.** This drink aids the brain's production of gamma-aminobutyric acid, a chemical that helps regulate nerve cells associated with anxiety. It's also used to treat insomnia, so this is best enjoyed right before bed.

2. **Matcha.** Matcha is like coffee's greener and more chill cousin. The caffeine in it provides sustained energy without the jitters. Matcha also contains L-theanine, which is known to boost your mood and relax your mind.

3. **Reishi mushrooms.** Also called "nature's Xanax," this powdered fungus is believed to improve sleep quality, inflammation, anxiety, and depression. Basically, if you're looking for some drinkable calm, then this is the drink for you.

4. **Anti-anxiety smoothies.** Try adding avocado (vitamin B for the brain), chia seeds (magnesium for stress management), almond butter (zinc and protein for anxiety control), or cacao (polyphenols for serotonin production) to add some chill to your blended-up bliss.

#58 Take a Bath

Bubble-bath babes, hot-water fiends, and sixty-minute-shower sisters, RISE UP! Your years of soap collecting and commitment to scorching hot water are finally getting the recognition they fucking deserve.

From Germany to Japan, multiple studies show that relaxing in your tub improves sleep quality, lowers tension, and even changes the chemicals in your brain, because a warm bath increases serotonin and decreases cortisol. In other words: yes, you can literally soak some of your troubles away.

Whether you are a standing-shower purist or a bastion of bathing (rubber ducky and all), each of us would benefit from getting a little hot and steamy in the bathroom and indulging in a bath bomb or six—strictly for your health, of course.

BOOST THAT BATH POTENTIAL

1. **Get steamy.** According to Science™, the perfect temperatures for a relaxing bath-time experience are a warm 105 degrees Fahrenheit for the water and a cool 77 degrees for the room. This sexy combo gently raises your body temperature, and the steam stimulates endorphin production. But hey, we're not here to turn tub time into temp-the-shit-out-of-the-water time. Let your body tell you what feels good—it knows its shit.

2. **Ban all electricity.** Relaxing bath time means Cozy Vibes Only (turn to page 154 to learn more about upping your hygge game). So swap overhead lighting for candles or

choose a book over your phone. Banning things that need power turns down the literal and metaphorical lights in your brain, and it opens up the peaceful space you need to quiet your anxious thoughts and unclench your muscles.

3. **Treat yourself.** Chances are that you try to be Extra-Extra in every aspect of your life, so why not go HAM for the self-care part, too? Try these goodies to reach your Relaxed-As-Fuck potential:

- Scented candles
- Bath bombs or salts
- Gentle body scrub
- Sheet mask
- Organic loofah
- Bubble bath with essential oils
- Hydrating hair mask
- Relaxing music
- Bathtub tray
- Wineglass holder

#59 Massage Your Hands

Look at your hands. What do you see? If your answer is something like "murder mittens ready to strangle the nearest Karen," then all right! We always stan, passionate sister. But you know what's also in those killer claws? A whole lot of tension that's probably causing you more pain than you realize. According to a study done in 2017, a regular hand massage can alleviate arthritis, reduce high blood pressure, and significantly reduce stress levels. So, take a five-minute break to relax your fist with a restorative massage.

A FIVE-MINUTE MASSAGE FOR YOUR MITTS

1. Sit in a comfortable place. Take your palm and rub your forearm from wrist to elbow. Massage back and forth at least three times on both sides of the forearm.
2. Using your palm again, rub your hand, moving from wrist to fingertips. Repeat three times for each side of your hand.
3. Place your hand on your forearm and wrap your thumb around to the underside of your arm. Starting at the wrist, squeeze your arm and release, all the way up and down.
4. Put your thumb on your palm, and place your pointer finger on the back of your hand. Take both fingers to rub circular or back-and-forth motions into your hand. Work your way up to your forearm; repeat three times.
5. Use your thumb and apply pressure all over your palm in a circular motion. Do the same for the back of your hand.
6. Rub your thumb from the base to the tip of each finger. Then massage the space between each finger.

Turn on Music

When the right song hits, your mood can change completely in the span of one advertisement (I'm looking at you, sob-fest SPCA commercials). Well, music grips our feelz because it takes the entire brain to decode a singular tune. Whether it's Britney or Beethoven, your brain is busting its ass to understand what the hell is going on: your cerebellum is processing the rhythm, and both frontal lobes are documenting the emotional signals. Spas and malls use that musical mind-hack to boost the feel-good hormones and lower adrenaline and cortisol (aka liquid stress) in your emotional mainframe. A good playlist can help you reenergize, wind down, or whatever else you need, and making your own can start like this.

HOW TO CREATE A THERAPEUTIC PLAYLIST

1. **Play what you love.** Always pick songs that fucking speak to you. Choose some of your most played tracks because chances are you really connect with them (bonus points for including anthems from your *angsty* teen phase).
2. **Match the vibe.** Think about the vibe you want to channel, then consider a song's tempo, volume, and lyrics. Shortcut your way to more energy with a marathon of upbeat bangers, or chill out with some groovy 70s hits.
3. **Build up the mood.** Try using music to build an emotional ladder, one that gradually moves you from the emotion you're feeling toward the one you want. Or, if you want to just feel your feelings, switch on a playlist that helps you rage-sing out all your anger or sob-croon out all your tears.

#61 Go Outside

Do you spend all day sitting in a box and staring at a glow-y box? Of course you do. We all live in twenty-first-century America, where your brain has a tantrum if it doesn't get constant digital entertainment. Other than the lack of fresh air, sunlight, nature, and even a hint of perspective, our perpetual life indoors isn't so bad once you get used to feeling like you're going batshit crazy.

Unfortunately, we have been informed that reading online articles about forest bathing and googling "cabin in the woods" is not the same thing to your brain as actually going outside. Studies show that even just twenty minutes outside can reduce stress hormones, up our happy chemicals, and help us feel recharged. But it is also pretty fucking boring if you just stand there doing nothing. So, here are a few chill ways to fit in your daily field trip.

FOUR WAYS TO GET UP AND GET OUT

1. **Eat outside.** You have to eat at least three times a day, so why not commandeer a park bench, squat on a curb, lie in a bush—we don't fucking care, as long as it feels good.
2. **Watch the sky.** Lying on a blanket + staring at the sky = tranquil as fuck.
3. **Hit up a park, any park.** Dog parks. State parks. Theme parks. Botanical gardens. The options go on and on, so pick one you like and get that tushy unparked off that couch.
4. **Go for a ten-minute walk.** Even a few minutes outside can clear your head, reframe your perspective, and keep you from slapping people you hate.

Talk to One of Your People #62

We know, we know. "Talk it out"? That's scary as fuck. But it's also more beneficial for your mind and body than you would think. Researchers at UCLA found that putting intense emotions (like fear, anger, and anxiety) into words moves the processing of those feelings from the amygdala (Panic Central) to more logical areas of the brain (the departments of Keep Calm and Carry On). All of this is great, but we know getting started can be its own anxiety hurdle, so here are a few tips to get you over the hump.

TALK IT OUT RIGHT OUT OF YOUR BRAIN

1. **Pick the right person.** You should obviously pick someone you trust. Less obviously, you should pick someone with the emotional energy to listen with the attention you deserve. So, always ask your person if they have space for you in their own emotional dumpster fire before you start sharing.

2. **Find a therapist.** A therapist might be the best option because it's their literal job to help you sort through your crap. For more info on finding the right therapist for you, flip to "How to Find a Dazzling Therapist" on page 57.

3. **Know when to stop.** You probably won't find a solution in one conversation, so take a break if you're feeling frustrated or stuck in a loop.

4. **Remember the good and the bad.** Talking about the bad is key to venting but remembering the good is key to actually feeling better, and it can be the turning point you need to save a crappy situation.

#63 Stretch

We're all aware that the brain controls the body, but would you believe that the body influences the brain just as much? Well, it's true. Physical movement or the lack thereof (desk workers, represent!) affects the brain's magical concoction of chemicals called Your Emotions. Basically, your brain AND your body could unite forces and create the greatest anxiety shit-storm you've ever seen, all from the comfort of your office chair.

This brain-body connection may be the biggest metaphorical and physical pain in the ass you've ever had, but a solution is literally within reach. Even if it's just reaching for your toes, stretching is just enough movement to break up the toxic tension pent up in your muscles and reset your mental and bodily mood! So, take a few minutes to give yourself the mind-body reset you need and try some of these simple stretches below.

THREE STRETCHES
TO REACH YOUR BEST SELF

Upper Back

1. While seated, extend your arms forward and clasp your hands together.
2. Tuck in your chin and round your back.
3. Reach your arms forward. Tighten your abs to intensify the stretch.
4. Hold for thirty seconds and repeat two or three times.

Chest and Shoulders

1. Clasp your hands behind your back.
2. Straighten your arms and gently lift your hands toward the ceiling. Try exhaling while doing this movement.
3. Hold for fifteen to thirty seconds and enjoy the comfortable pull in your chest and shoulders. Repeat two or three times.

Quads

1. Stand next to a wall or another surface that can be used to keep your balance.
2. Shift your weight to your right leg. Bend your left knee so your foot is behind you.
3. Use your left hand to grab the top of your foot. You will feel a pull along your left thigh.
4. Hold for thirty seconds and then switch sides. Repeat for both sides two or three times.

153

#64 Get Cozy

According to happiness researchers, Denmark is home to some of the happiest people on Earth. Their concept of "hygge" (pronounced "hoo-guh") takes the happiness you get from reading a good book with a warm drink and a fluffy blanket and turns it into a whole lifestyle. Hygge is all about doing the things you enjoy with people you like in a comforting and safe environment. Even better: the Danes' cozy way of living has been linked to higher optimism, stronger self-compassion, and lower depression, stress, and anxiety. This is because of the mind-body connection, which links your physical condition to your mental well-being. In other words, another fuzzy throw won't cure an anxiety wildfire, but it can damn well snuff out some smaller stress sparks.

D.I.Y. YOUR OWN SNUGGERY

1. **It's all about the ambiance.** Atmosphere is key, so harsh fluorescent lights and overhead fixtures are O.U.T., out. Use floor and table lamps to set a more intimate mood, and don't be afraid to fire up a candle or two.

2. **Embrace soft textures.** If you need another excuse to refresh your stock of fluffy blankets, pillows, rugs, and throws, then this is it. Soft textures and materials are tactile soothers that add to a room's calm and cozy vibe.

3. **Foster meaningful connections.** Hygge is about warming the body AND the heart. This means doing things that make you happy with people who bring you joy. So, host a casual game night or coffee get-together and invite only people you like—not the assholes—into your cozy sanctuary.

Eat a Snack #65

Have you ever seen a toddler throw the most EPIC of tantrums but then be perfectly fine at the drop of those magic words, "It's snack time!"? Well, your anxiety IS that toddler. Your stress hormones (yay, cortisol!) trigger two world-shaking emergency functions in your body: the fight-or-flight response and "hanger" with a capital ANGER. When cortisol attacks, your blood sugar plummets and peaces out faster than your willpower. In fact, cortisol makes you crave carbs even more than usual because carbs are the fastest way to raise your blood sugar back up to yeah-I'm-okay-now levels.

Which means we should talk about some ways to snack better. Dietitians recommend starting a snack session with something that will sustain a stable blood-sugar level (i.e. food with fats, protein, and fiber) so you don't fall prey to a sugar crash. So, next time your anxiety goes into brat mode, give it one of these options.

SNACK YOUR ANXIETY AWAY

1. **Protein.** Whether it's jerky, peanut butter, or a handful of nuts, protein will level out your feelz realz fast. Scope your snack aisle for portable proteins.

2. **Leafy greens.** Green veggies give your body a healthy dose of folate, a vitamin that may help with your body's production of dopamine. Try flavored kale chips or green smoothies for an on-the-go salad-ish experience.

3. **Dark chocolate.** Research shows that dark chocolate actually reduces cortisol and relaxes blood vessels (meaning, lowers blood pressure). And when they say dark, they mean dark, so we recommend 70 percent cocoa or higher.

#66 Journal

Some people compare anxiety to "an emotional rollercoaster ride," and those people are full of bullshit. Anxiety isn't about highs and lows. It's more like a rickety-ass carnival ride that slams you against the wall and spins you until you want to puke your guts out.

The Anxiety Spiral is the ultimate ride from hell because it scrambles your thoughts so much that finding the exit can feel fucking impossible. Well, step right up, folks! This freakshow of stress and suckiness may seem overwhelming, but we're about to whip some discipline back into this circus with the power of the pen.

A journal is more than just a place to dump a problem's ass—it's your space to reflect and regroup. Journaling can help put things into perspective, document how your thinking works, and track patterns that trigger anxious phases. Finding your style can take time, but right now, the point is to just give it a little teensy try. So take just fifteen minutes for a straight-up, no-bullshit brain dump.

FUCK-THAT-SHIT FREEWRITING

1. Set a timer for fifteen to twenty minutes.
2. Write everything that comes to mind and don't stop writing. No one is grading your grammar or spelling, so write without worrying about making mistakes.
3. Keep going. If you run out of things to say, then write about that. Keep producing words until the timer buzzes.
4. Review your writing after the timer goes off. Notice what jumps out at you. Some people like to write a few lines at the end to summarize what they found important.

Read a Book #67

Why should you read a book? Well, to put it tactfully, the real world sucks ass, and you need an escape from it. But reading is more than just an emergency I-gotta-get-the-fuck-outta-here button. It may be the best way to kick anxiety's ass. Researchers have seen that as little as six minutes of reading can lower stress by 60 percent. That's roughly 70 percent better than music and about 300 percent better than walking. Reading gives us greater perspective, refreshing escapism, and stronger empathy (even toward ourselves!). So, try out these tips to help you channel your bookworm energy.

HOW TO FIND YOUR NEXT READ

1. **Follow your interests.** Reading to take your mind off of anxious thoughts means that you have to ACTUALLY LIKE WHAT YOU'RE READING. Anxiety is looking for any chance to derail your focus, so pick a book you can't put down.

2. **Think outside the text box.** If you'd rather stare at a blank wall than read a page of solid words, then you don't have to fucking do it. Because news flash: this isn't high school English class, and books don't have to be straight text. Try a graphic novel, or an illustrated classic, or an audiobook.

3. **Check out staff recommendations.** People who work with books are like vegans: they're very picky about what they consume, and they want to tell you all about it. So why not humor them the next time you walk into a bookstore?

4. **Let a robot pick.** Websites, like Gnooks.com, recommend new books based on the ones you already like, with ZERO human interaction. That's the kind of futurist shit we live for.

#68 Watch Something

You know when you're stressed about how much you have to do and so you decide to get started by speed running all twenty-two seasons of *Law & Order: Special Victims Unit*? And how it doesn't make any fucking sense, but you do it anyway? Hell yeah.

Studies have found that re-watching shows we like can reenergize us and actually help us perform better on challenging tasks. Some researchers believe that re-watching lowers our stress because we know what's coming and raises our positive hormones because we're in a space that makes us happy.

So, yes, you should watch some TV when you need a pick-me-up, but you do want to do it in a way that feels good and not like more garbage on your plate. Follow these tips and optimize your thirty to sixty minutes in televised heaven.

TIPS FOR HEALTHY TV TIME

1. **Check that tone.** Watch what you enjoy, but try to notice the show's tone. We all love a good true crime documentary, but a comedy or rom-com is probably more likely to lift your mood, if that's what you need right then.

2. **Choose sprints over marathons.** "Moderation" is the name of the game. Like anything, too much TV is a no-go for better health. So, break up your tube time with exercise, chores, or anything else that doesn't involve a screen.

3. **Remember your social life.** Even though they say they don't, your friends really want to hear about what happened on your shows. Trust us.

Try a New Hobby #69

Here's the big ol' truth: you should pick up a new hobby because Science and Research say so. According to a 2016 study published in *The Journal of Positive Psychology,* people who work on a creative hobby every day reported higher levels of psychological well-being than those who didn't. 'Nough said—let's get fucking to it.

FOUR HOBBIES TO TEST DRIVE

1. **Chef it up.** Listen, you need to eat anyway, and apparently getting into the kitchen can be really calming? And no, you don't have to be the best chef or go from zero kitchen time to a month-long sourdough starter. Like all of these anxiety-busting activities, what really matters is just trying.

2. **Find a way to move that you don't hate.** There's just no way around it (trust us, we tried): exercise is good for breaking up all the built-up stress-crud in our lives. So, try our five-minute yoga routine on page 39, or walk up the street (to get ice cream)—do whatever will get you moving.

3. **Become a plant mom.** Plants are a lot like us: they feel emotions, thrive with a little TLC, and love a good drink. Any type of philodendron or cactus is a great place to start because they're tough as fuck and love being indoors.

4. **Find anything creative that you could get into.** Painting, photography, music, writing, hand-lettering, embroidery, take your pick! Say "no" to soul-crushing worry, and say "yes" to another adult coloring book (or try the color-by-numbers pages at the back of this book!).

#70 Take Time Off

Grappling with anxiety is a lot like boxing: it's brutal, intense, and kinda sweaty in an icky way. And just like any prizefighter, you keep getting up. But every once in a while, your opponent lands one precise uppercut that puts you down for the count.

After anxiety's knocked you down, it's going to take a hell of a lot more than a splash of water to the face to get you back on your feet, and that's okay. Because taking a breather from the boxing ring of Everyday Bullshit is the beginning of your comeback. Taking a mental health day or week, or even a sabbatical, might just be the reset you need, and these are some things you can do to optimize that time and come back stronger than ever before.

HOW TO RECHARGE AND RESET

1. **Focus on yourself.** This is YOU time. Not "agonize over Jerk A, B, or C" time or "fixate on a fear that will honestly probably never happen" time. So, catching up on emails, or running errands, or any other bullshit like this is banned. Your break time is all about doing what you need to do to feel better and get back to being the boss bitch you are.

2. **Set goals.** Lying on the couch can be part of your self-love vacay, but you'll need to get up eventually, too. Try setting small goals that will help improve your whole well-being, like cooking a healthy meal, calling a friend, or exercising.

3. **Prioritize self-care.** When coming back after a rough scuffle with anxiety, you still have to train and get stronger, just in a different way. Self-care is that training, and it will help you recharge your bullshit-tolerance reservoirs.

Laugh  #71

People say, "Laughter is the best medicine," and—we can't believe we're saying this—those cheese doodles are right. A good laugh decreases stress, relaxes muscles, boosts the immune system, and increases endorphins. Laughing more is like building a new habit; the more you practice it, the more you'll start doing it without trying.

HOW TO LAUGH IN ANXIETY'S STUPID FACE

1. **Spend time with un-shitty, upbeat people.** Have you noticed how you're more likely to LOL if you're with another person? That's because laughter is infectious. So, surround yourself with people who love to laugh because they probably also love to see you smile, and that's a win-win.

2. **Find a podcast that makes you giggle like a weirdo.** There are hundreds of comedy podcasts out there, so you'll never run out of material or reasons to laugh in public like the crazy person you might actually be.

3. **Create a meme mecca of a pinterest board.** The internet's greatest gift to the world wasn't faster communication or better access to information—it was meme culture. Sometimes it only takes a few high-quality memes or clips to crack your funk, and Pinterest is the perfect place to curate your giggle-inducing hoard of top-tier internet humor.

4. **Cheer up your sad-ass space.** You know what's not fun? Being stuck in a yawn of a room. So, spruce up your space with goofy things, like a photo with your friends or a piece of wall art with a dorky phrase, even if you're laughing *at* it. Live, laugh, love, right?!

#72 Take a Nap

You know when something tech-y breaks, and the first thing they tell you to do is to unplug it, wait ten seconds, then plug it back in? And ridiculously, it works, like, 95 percent of the time? Naps are that for your body and brain. That's because a nap is the equivalent of shutting down your operating system for a few minutes and then powering back up in a calmer, less glitch-y way. Sleep experts have found that even a ten to twenty minute power nap can reduce stress, improve perception, brighten your mood, boost memory, increase creativity, aid in weight loss, enhance your sex life, and make your hair look fucking unbelievable.*

So whether your day was off to a shitty start and you want a Groundhog Day re-do, you can't turn off the panicky thoughts and roiling anxiety, or you're just kind of over it all and could use a self-imposed attitude adjustment, a nap is the answer.

Don't know how to make a nap fit into a bonkers day? First, throw out the idea that you need a lot of time to nap or that you need to fully fall asleep during your nap. Nope. A nap can just be closing your eyes and resting your body for a few minutes without falling asleep. A nap can be as short as ten minutes of slouching in a chair, shutting your eyes, and focusing on your breathing (see page 48 if you're like "WTF how?"). Or a nap can be twenty or thirty minutes of kicking the seat back in your car and power-snoozing in the parking lot. Whatever it is, this is your time, and you have full permission to hide from, ghost, or push back anyone or anything that gets in the way.

HOW TO FIGHT FOR YOUR RIGHT TO NAP

1. Figure out how much time you can steal for yourself. Plead illness if you have to. Remember that saying "no" is one of the purest forms of self-love (see page 64 for how to swat away dumb people and their dumb demands).

2. Find a quiet place away from people, or create your own little nap den by snuggling deep into your clothing and popping in headphones. Having an oversized scarf, hooded sweater, or other cozy bit of clothing on hand can work wonders to hide you from annoying people who want your time.

3. Shut your eyes, breathe, and let a soft smile come to your lips. Ahhh. You're safe behind those eyelids. No one can get you here. This is your ten—maybe twenty—minutes to just breathe and be.

4. If you think you might fall asleep, set an alarm on your phone so you don't have to worry about missing the next thing you need to get to. But even if you have more time, limit your nap to thirty or fourty-five minutes, as napping longer than that might make you groggy and cranky.

5. When the time is up, open your eyes and look around. It's all going to be okay. You're safe here on this planet, in this moment.

6. Go about your day with a happy sense of pride that you did something really nice for yourself. You're going to be okay, because you always have that safe private nap retreat within you.

7. Repeat every damn day if you feel like it, because life is too short to reboot everything but yourself.

*That last one is Future Science, i.e., we made it up.

CHAPT

hush up–it's time for

Shh. It's shutty uppy time.

CHAPTER SIX

your daily moment of zen

#73 Sweet Silence, or Podcasts, for Your Moment of Zen

Listen . . . no, like, actually pause for a few seconds and take in the sounds around you. We are bombarded by a whole soundboard of noise from the moment our alarms bitch-slap our eyes open. The constant beeps and boops or dings and buzzes that you write off as background noise are actually an endless stream of data that your brain has to process whether you notice it or not.

Basically, if total silence were water, your mind would be the motherfucking Sahara Desert (that's zero to three inches of rainfall PER YEAR, by the way). Research shows that a regular dose of complete silence calms us and may even help renew our brain cells. And things like walks, yoga, or meditation are top-tier ways to give you and your mind some refuge from the auditory clusterfuck that you usually endure.

But wait—what about those moments when you can't even hear the external world over the internal scream-fest known as the Anxiety Spiral? Well, we move to Plan B, aka Operation Drown Out The Bullshit. This code-red tactical strike has a singular objective: break the anxious thought pattern as quickly as possible.

A grounding technique is usually our first line of defense, but if that's not doing it, we're not above an old-fashioned diversion, like a podcast, to stem the stream of inner screaming. To your brain, tuning in to a podcast is like flashing a piece of bacon in front of a drooling doggo—it immediately forgets almost everything else in the universe but the thing in front of it.

Besides drawing the mind away from your internal crapola, podcasts teach you new information AND leave your hands and eyes available for other things. May we suggest a loving hand massage or some veggie chopping?

Need some suggestions? Well, guess who's got you. It's us! Like a fine wine, these podcasts pair well with equally sophisticated activities, like strolling to the snack drawer, coloring (imperfectly) inside the lines, or couch-potato-ing like a champ.

QUIRKY

"The Infinite Monkey Cage" by the BBC for a witty and tongue-in-cheek take on some profound topics about our universe.

SELF-HELP

"The Positive Psychology Podcast" by Kristen Truempy for strategies on how to tackle mindfulness, self-love, and more.

"The Hardcore Self Help Podcast with Duff the Psych" by Robert Duff, PhD, for a no-bullshit, easily understandable take on complex self-help topics.

SLEEP

"Sleep with Me" by Night Vale Presents for lulling stories with just the right amount of sleep-inducing monotone.
"The New Yorker: Fiction" with Deborah Treisman for a grown-up bedtime story.

MEDITATION

"Meditation Minis Podcast" by Chel Hamilton for ten minutes of guided meditation.
"Happy Place" by Fearne Cotton for learning the secrets of happiness from a variety of unique and inspiring guests.

MENTAL + PHYSICAL HEALTH

"The Anxiety Podcast" by Tim JP Collins for tips on managing anxiety.
"Science Vs" by Gimlet Media for a myth-busting analysis of trending health, fitness, and science fads.

FUNNY

"The Shit Show" by Shit You Should Care About for a "Dear Abby"-style advice program, but with a hell of a lot more cursing.

Calligraphy for People with Shitty Handwriting

You know what's relaxingly retro? Writing things by hand. There's something about holding a pen and scratching it across paper that reminds us to slow down, set aside the screens, and start really seeing things. That is, unless what you're seeing is garbage handwriting, and you can't for fuck's sake read what you wrote.

If that's you, you've found your home: welcome to a mini-course in "Calligraphy for People with Shitty Handwriting." (Even if you have nice handwriting [jealousy glare], we can teach you how to make it suck here.) Crappy Calligraphy is to handwriting what the inflatable dancing dude outside of car dealerships is to ballet. We're about to get ZaNy and loose up in here!

The point here is to *feel* your writing. Whatever each mantra brings out in you each time you write it, let that emotion flow through the pen or pencil and onto the paper, making the letters reflect what you feel inside. Pissed off? Stab the paper like the fucking asshole that it is. Zen-ed out? Stroke that pencil lovingly across the paper. Whatever you're feeling, it's not wrong and it's always right. So put the phone down, turn on some tunes (see page 149 for ideas), and write it all out on the following pages.

I believe in good.

_____

_____

_____

_____

_____

_____

I am 100 percent That Bitch.

_____

_____

_____

_____

_____

I am strong *and* soft.

_____

_____

_____

_____

_____

I can use my anger for CHANGE.

_____

_____

_____

_____

I am loved.

_____

_____

_____

_____

_____

_____

I can forgive myself and others.

_____

_____

_____

_____

_____

Peace-In, Peace-Out #80

```
P Q S F S I F Q E S C P M J Z J B E
R E E M Z S U H X T Z E Y O G C R L
O Q A Y H I E P U B D S P Y Q C P I
S X Q C E S F N T B T O W C J V E C
A Z F T E E S F L G W P O Y B T P N
W E R W T V K R A L I E E L A X X O
Y T I D I C A L P I I R E I C H V C
H I X F R J S Q V C Y T V H C A C E
Q Y S Z B U A Y F T N E S E I Y L R
G X M B D D D V I L L Z M Q X X J M
M X O N O B T L X L G A M U S F D K
I Q J X X S I N A N O I O A D D R H
K X M H E U S I L E N C E N A G C A
M I U R Q N K X M F H E W I M V T R
H S X N E H T O O S M H R M F S R M
H K A S E R E N I T Y R T I D T G O
M R D A J M E Z J J B X W T Z U R N
T G S A O H E T N A U C B Y U D Y Y
```

tranquility	quiet	rest	hush
serenity	placidity	silence	soothe
peace	stillness	calm	reconcile
harmony	repose	equanimity	alleviate

#81 Indoor Forest-Bathing

```
G M O U J A R J B K W R E A Y W K Y
X I T T H Z P F V J R E V E O X E V
U D I T S K F V M Q S U I N R O C K
W K M W U S C V C T K L S A N T T H
N W Q X Z M A N C D C W D A B R Y Y
I L K R I S B R U N X K N C K F R Y
S C G E X B N S G I E I R T U R B Z
Q O A K L X A S Y W M Q C D H O C S
A O I U K E E K O A J A T U X W U Y
C E Y L O R C Y L L K L S Y J A T I
I L L V B F O Z Y A D R S U N S E T
K V O G B K T K S B E N I H S N U S
W N A U D J G U E V H J G P B K A M
X U B S D R O G I K P Q C Q H G V L
R R O R A N K R K S L H G O M W J F
T B T I M R L I M S E P E Z E E O Q
W P N U L K I E X J A U W B V V X N
E W J W K R E W O L F A U R Z W R G
```

flower	rock	sunshine	sunset
tree	cloud	grass	soil
ocean	sky	wind	leaf
river	rain	snow	animal

It's the Little Things

```
S I U D K S W E Y J B U C W T B Y W
A T C Z E L K O K F J O I X Y Z R K
C Z K O O B G L V Y F L N V H J H J
Z K R S J A A R I A V C C C Z O O X
P G V G P W M E B S D M I V D A Z W
U N U A B K V V X O G E P R O C T Q
H I N H W O U D L K E C B X P H J R
M T K X Y G O D E L O O G J J N A L
S U X H P M M S D S P F N S B X V Q
S Y S F Z O A N O J S F N L L T X N
I G J I V V A F L O W E R S A P A N
L A B I C C N T Y J Z E R W N I Z K
C Z E O E K E W G V M R A T K H I R
X Z L I A U J C A F N L D S E V I L
U I Q G N C B Q B B D M Z Y T U L F
W P G W B B P W F U Z U C Y L C Q B
B B C H F Y J X M R L V X O Z U V U
V Z H J O B A T H P K K D G A I Q G
```

candle	yoga pants	walk	old movie
bath	book	flowers	nap
dessert	bed	music	hug
blanket	pizza	coffee	picnic

#83 Meet Empowered You

```
X X T K S A H M T R K C G J N W N F
W A B Q G O A O N P G A R Q H H B U
Y J F O K K K Y A A L Q F O R E L C
C R E A T I V E I S C B V A C G I S
L T N A I D A R L S Y S G N R T U H
L F G V N W H C L I K X S M E O V C
U U V N O G D H I O C R B G E N D I
I K F R I X A H R N T Z R G F C J T
C M T E B L Q S B A U E A C I O P E
U H A F S Y L O P T N R Z M E E T N
Y B J G Y O F E A E U W H H R C T G
P W Q O I Y P K P O Q Q Y S C V Y A
P Y J B R N G R C M B V I Q E B B M
C F F X R C A Q U Y O S P E P B B F
G F J G S A Z T L P T C R N L K H H
O C G N I N V U I E L U F R E W O P
H N T U H U Y E N V L U M I N O U S
H M X F P Q V T Y I E V K I E H Y Z
```

passionate	brilliant	fierce	magnetic
worthy	courageous	persistent	energetic
radiant	creative	powerful	luminous
purposeful	brave	compelling	imaginative

Salve for Your Wounds

```
H  P  S  I  D  B  G  T  I  N  X  R  W  R  N  E  N  E
U  T  A  S  Z  K  R  B  O  X  D  L  E  C  D  A  P  C
C  S  M  U  E  O  U  I  A  E  U  Q  B  L  Z  S  S  N
N  K  P  R  F  N  T  U  G  B  I  V  W  U  I  E  B  A
Z  A  Q  M  A  A  T  S  S  E  N  T  F  O  S  E  K  R
T  A  O  P  X  W  Y  E  K  G  N  Y  C  H  Y  D  F  U
C  C  T  A  A  U  S  P  I  W  O  O  W  V  T  I  M  S
X  U  L  P  E  A  C  E  U  U  N  A  G  H  I  O  T  S
A  E  C  A  Y  T  Z  Q  G  T  Q  A  U  C  R  G  C  A
R  Z  L  S  V  L  K  U  E  K  U  X  X  O  U  F  J  E
V  S  I  W  V  C  R  N  H  S  C  A  D  Z  C  P  Y  R
I  Q  S  Q  K  T  T  G  T  Y  H  L  M  I  E  B  N  L
C  A  L  M  W  M  Y  Q  X  X  M  B  L  N  S  E  Y  G
B  L  M  C  E  R  P  Y  Y  L  L  O  K  E  S  U  J  R
W  M  P  N  N  E  E  V  B  I  Y  O  K  S  X  S  T  G
V  A  T  U  H  S  V  S  S  D  L  J  H  S  R  H  H  B
P  V  Y  T  E  F  A  S  T  Z  P  F  V  I  F  E  B  T
A  P  B  U  B  X  Y  Z  X  P  P  F  Q  C  T  K  Z  P
```

relaxation	bliss	comfort	contentment
calm	softness	peace	safety
relief	warmth	rest	quietness
ease	reassurance	coziness	security

#85 I Really Love You

```
G B R C P P A A V J P C O Q G U G T
L H N F V R Y G D A T C E P S E R H
D E V O T I O N S M T N U H N Y K O
N S I K Y V C S E H I J I O Q E Z U
R O O Z Y Z I K A O V R I Z J S B G
H C I U S O V M W N I T A W D N N H
O P O T N W N W R O A W Q T W E R T
A D R Y A F F E P R E T R W I L U F
S F I A N I V E E U D H K S P O N U
T N F F W E C D Y A C G J N T A N L
R E S E R E I E L G E I M U Z D A N
T Q Y E C S P C R C E L K G Y O F E
S T N G N T X R H P Y E G T A R Y S
H C O O I L I J G C P D L I F A F S
E W C A W D E O N U U A U L R T C Q
V E N J O Y M E N T Y Y C T T I F F
K I N D N E S S T O U F H F U O T R
T I C E I F E P L I O F J H P N X P
```

devotion	respect	enjoyment	consideration
affection	appreciation	admiration	kindness
honor	delight	thoughtfulness	awe
passion	loyalty	reverence	adoration

A Stroll Through a Labyrinth for the Lazy

#86 #91

The labyrinth is an ancient maze that lets you turn inward, and it can help you look at a question from different angles until you finally arrive at its central truth. If that sounds woo-woo, it's because, yeah, there's some mystical magic in this weird little maze! The great thing about a labyrinth is that it doesn't make you choose directions, so it lets your mind wander as you "walk" along it.

Try to trace these labyrinths in a quiet spot, where you can have a few minutes of monastic-like silence and solitude. First, think of a question. Then, move your pen or pencil along the labyrinth as slowly as humanly possible. We're talking snail crawl. Focus on the scrape of your pen or pencil along the paper. Your entire universe right now is moving this pen slowly along this path. Yes, it's weird. As you go, let your mind wander anywhere it wants along the contours of the question. Each time your mind wanders off, pull it gently back, like how you're pulling the pencil gently along the paper.

When you're done, jot down anything that came up, even if it was a partial thought, a next question to ask, an unexpected emotion, or the answer itself. How did it feel? Did your mind like having a few minutes of silence, or did it try to run away to a thousand sparkly things, or both? Whatever it was, just notice it. It's all good. Even though all of the labyrinth paths here are the same, you'll have a totally different experience each time, depending on the question and your frame of mind. But we are going to be cheesy and just say it: may these labyrinth paths bring you a teensy smidge of peace for whatever you do next. Amen, girlfren.

_____
_____
_____
_____
_____
_____
_____
_____
_____
_____
_____
_____
_____

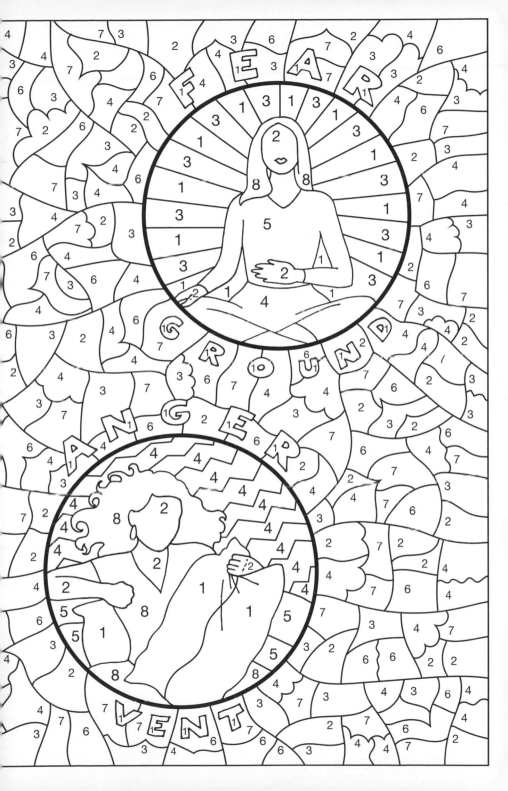

Solutions

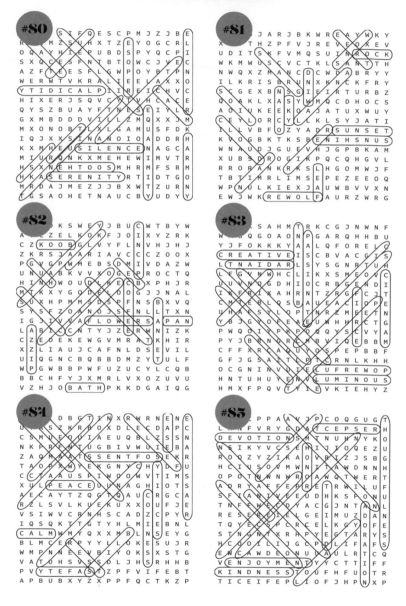

Resources

Just like getting glammed up is all about having the right products, taking care of your mental health is all about finding and using the right tools and practices. You were born beautiful, but because we were all born a little zany, remember that asking for help during tough times makes you a smart and strong human, not someone needy. Here are tools and organizations that are standing at the ready to make your life better and easier anytime you need it.

MENTAL HEALTH APPS

Talkspace
MindShift
Breathe2Relax
Stress & Anxiety Companion
Stop, Breathe & Think

WEBSITES AND ONLINE SUPPORT

National Institute of Mental Health
IMAlive
MentalHealth.gov
National Alliance on Mental Illness
Anxiety and Depression Association of America

HOTLINES

National Suicide Prevention Lifeline: 1-800-273-8255
Samaritans Crisis Hotline: 1-877-870-4673
Obsessive Compulsive Anonymous Nationwide Conference Call:
1-712-432-0075

Acknowledgments

We're taking our own advice and sending all the gratitude ever to our families, friends, and the therapists that help us stay family and friends. Special thanks to Carolina Ribas, for being the kind of sister every girl should have and for just *getting* it. A huge thank you to Claire Lewis, who is the kind of dazzling therapist who can, like, *actually* change a life.

Immense thanks to Carson Watlington, Alexis Seabrook, and Natallia Babusko for contributing their snappy words and stunning art to this book. An equally giant "thank you" to Maria Ribas and the team at Stonesong and Allison Adler and the team at Andrews McMeel An equally giant "thank you" to Maria Ribas and the team at Stonesong and Allison Adler, Meg Daniels, Diane Marsh, Tamara Haus, and the team at Andrews McMeel. Thanks for making this book real and keepin' it real the whole way through.